THE
PHILOSOPHER'S
JOKE

Frontiers of Philosophy

Peter H. Hare, Series Editor

Advisory Board

THE
PHILOSOPHER'S
JOKE

ESSAYS IN
FORM AND
CONTENT

RICHARD A. WATSON

PROMETHEUS BOOKS
BUFFALO, NEW YORK

Published 1990 by Prometheus Books
With editorial offices located at
700 East Amherst Street, Buffalo, New York 14215,
and distribution facilities at
59 John Glenn Drive, Amherst, New York 14228.

Library of Congress Cataloging-in-Publication Data

Watson, Richard A., 1931-
    The philosopher's joke: essays in form and content / by Richard A. Watson
        p.   cm.—(Frontiers of philosophy)
    Includes bibliographical references
    ISBN 0-87975-601-2 (alk. paper)
    1. Form (Philosophy) 2. Hylomorphism. 3. Philosophy—Humor.
4. Literature—Philosophy. I. Title. II. Series.
B945.W295P45 1990
100—dc20   90-38430
                                                                 CIP

Printed on acid-free paper in the United States of America

A Note From The Series Editor

The pieces by Richard Watson collected in this volume are un-conventional in important respects. Although they contain, among other things, philosophical arguments on fundamental issues, they are written with an attention to style—philosophical as much as literary—not found in conventional philosophical writing. Such concern with matters of style, while the most interesting and original aspect of the book, is likely to be what most unsettles philosophers who expect a book to have a uniform logical structure. It should be pointed out that, although Watson's essays are intended to be literature as much as philosophy, they are not meant to be dismissive of philosophy. Through humor Watson wishes to make his readers aware of philosophical content as well as form.

Peter H. Hare

Acknowledgments

I much enjoyed and benefitted from discussion of fine points with Stanley W. Lindberg, and Stephen Corey of *The Georgia Review,* Peter Davidson of the Atlantic Monthly Press, and Raymond L. Williams of the *Latin American Review.* I thank them and also the editors of *Methodos* for permission to reprint here in different form pieces that first appeared ~~in their journals~~ as follows:

"The Relation of Truth of Content to Perfection of Form in Literature," *Methodos* 15 (1963): 3–16.

"The Seducer and the Seduced," *The Georgia Review* 39 (1985): 353–366.

"How to Die," *The Georgia Review* 37 (1983): 307–316;

"Ape Dreams," *The Georgia Review* 41 (1987): 288–298.

"A Pig's Tail," *Latin American Review* 15 (1987): 89–91.

The Philosopher's Diet, Boston: Atlantic Monthly Press (1985): 136-150.

Preface

(After the Ball Is Over)

Professor Rhodes Dunlap, as luck would have it, had been a Rhodes Scholar, and he was head of the selection committee for Rhodes Scholarship candidates at The State University of Iowa. When he called me into his office in 1950, during my sophomore year, and offered to coach me for a Rhodes Scholarship competition if I would but enter the Honors Program in English, two thoughts came into my mind. First, I did not want to spend my life correcting freshman themes, and second, I had already noticed that English was taught by Amateur Philosophers—so why not major in The Real Thing under the guidance of Professionals?

But there was more to it than that. Earlier that year, on the basis of a short story I had turned in as a permitted alternative to writing a critical essay in a course called "Understanding Fiction" (Can you name the authors of the text?), Verlin Cassill had told me that I would be an outstanding Creative Writing major. You understand that this was like being offered encouragement in, say, The Piano on the one hand and Civil Engineering on the other, for at that time there was—and is even today, for all I know— a chasm in the English Department at Iowa between Literature and Creative Writing every bit as wide and deep as that between

9

Art and Science. My friend Frank Thompson was cast into this abyss because of his bizarre desire to write a regular English Literature dissertation on William Carlos Williams. The department elders (of whom Rhodes Dunlap was one) voted overwhelmingly that W. C. Williams was not a subject for a Literature degree, but was fit to be treated only by the Creative Writing faculty. Frank wrote his dissertation, but never got his degree.

I did not major in Creative Writing because I thought I did not (yet) have anything to say. I thought you had to know something to be a writer. I knew I had some grasp of form, but very little content. This scruple now seems to me to have been a charming aberration in A Young Man who admired Truman Capote's vacuous *Other Voices, Other Rooms,* and totally ridiculous given the average data base of many Writers I Have Known since. Alas, I fear that what was really present in my nearly empty mind was the expectation that if I majored in Philosophy I would learn something very important. I think I thought I would find out *What It All Means.*

Just what did I want to know? And did I find it? Well, I did not know what I was looking for, and nearly the first thing I found out was that if you do know what you are looking for, you already have it, and if you do not know what you are looking for, you will not be able to recognize it when you find it. I thought this was Pretty Funny, so despite the risk I went on in Philosophy. Soon enough The Quest In The West was revealed to be For Certainty. And before I could even ask, "Certainty About What?" Richard Popkin told me about Pyrrhonian Skepticism.

The Pyrrhonian Skeptic tries to maintain perfect peace of mind by suspending judgment on all things. To do this he raises counter-arguments to oppose and exactly balance all arguments for all positions. With no opinions, he lives tranquilly whatever transpires (for example, Nixon, Carter, Reagan, Bush), because he has not committed himself one way or the other. This is droll enough, but what if someone presents The Skeptic with an argument for which he cannot find a balancing counter-argument? Never fear, The Skeptic has A Killer Argument. He merely holds up the palms of his hands and says, "Ah, my friend, you seem to have me, but Think! I have but feeble wit. Perhaps someone else knows an argument against your position, and perhaps in the course of time even I will think of one. So, despite not being able to meet your argument at the moment, I must even so suspend judgment," et cetera, and so on.

The Skeptics are good for a lot of laughs, like the story that Pyrrho's disciples had to lead him around to keep him from Stepping In Dog Shit. (How did *they* know?)

I thought Philosophy was great sport, but I was heavy-handed. I learned what *finesse* was one day when Gustav Bergmann screamed at me, "God Damn It, Watson, you're supposed to do Philosophy with an épée, not a broadsword!" It is not classy to cut off your opponent's head; drawing one drop of blood from the tip of his nose will suffice. Here is an example:

During the Reformation both Catholics and Protestants used skeptical arguments against each other. The Catholics asked in particular how the Protestants could be sure that Calvin, say, or Luther, was not crazy, or even downright insane. Getting The Word From God, voices in their heads—that sort of thing is suspect, to say the least. Much better, the Catholics said, to stick with Tradition, with the well-considered and hallowed pronouncements of the Fathers of the Church. And, in particular, the Catholics could bank on the infallibility of the Pope for guidance.

In response, the Protestants said—and this illustrates the nice point about fine philosophical argument—that they would fully admit, For The Sake Of The Argument, that what the Catholics said could be true. But unfortunately, even if it was true, there remained one small problem. Suppose Tradition as established by the Fathers of the Church does tell the true way to Salvation, and suppose the infallible Pope interprets this Tradition perfectly. Even so, a question remains: Who is the Pope? I am a mere fallible human being, so I can never be certain that the man claiming to be the Pope *is* the Pope. And even if I knew who the Pope is, how could I, error-prone and none too bright, be sure I understand correctly what he says?

Sometimes a student laughs when I tell that story in class. To show my gratitude, I usually take the lad or lass aside and tell him or her that it probably would be best not to go on in Philosophy. This is Deadly Serious Stuff, and a robust sense of humor is apt to be detrimental to one's advancement.

The first Funny Philosophy I ever wrote is "The Relation of Truth of Content to Perfection of Form in Literature." I had started my teaching career at The University of Michigan and the colloquium committee of the English Department, those earnest Seekers After Truth (Some Of My Best Friends Are English Professors), had asked my colleague Frithjof Bergmann to give them a paper on that topic. He declined, as I recall, on the grounds that the topic was silly.

But no, I said, if your first name were only Gustav, you could write it. And having had many courses at Iowa from Gustav Bergmann, I bet Frithjof that I could write a paper on that topic, and, what is more, get it published. I won the bet with what I still think is the formally funniest piece in this volume, although if you prefer Slapstick to Deadpan, perhaps you had better read "Hopping and Skipping" first, to obtain an Ordinary Language Perspective with which to appreciate the absurdity of a rigid application of the Ideal Language Method to the bitter end. Of course Frithjof Got The Last Laugh. He got tenure and they fired me, or, as they still say in Academe with a straight face, they Let Me Go. This is something like the passing some people do instead of dying.

Which brings me to my suspicion of What Philosophy Is All About: Death. The Mortal Coil is wound tense in us all, but one day, sooner or later, it lets go with a Ge-Whang! and then You Are Dead. Why this should happen is A Puzzle To Everyone, despite the fact that the biological parameters are perfectly well understood by us all. The amazing thing is that most of us are surprised at a certain point in our lives to discover that It Really Is True, We Are *Indeed* (Philosophers use this word to indicate that Things Are Getting Serious and that They Really Mean What They Are About To Say) *Indeed* We Are Going To Die.

But I Will Get To That Later.

"The Relation of Truth of Content to Perfection of Form in Literature" is a mouth-filling period piece of The 1950s. Ye Olde Tyme Vienna Circle Logical Positivists did believe that with The Ideal Language Method they had Truth By The Tail. "Hopping and Skipping" celebrates the urgent, even frantic concern of many of the Oxford-Inspired Ordinary Language Philosophers during The 1960s, that this might not be the case. I wrote the piece under the inspiration of J. O. Urmson and Richard Cartwright while I was still (with them) at Michigan. It did not get published, but it got around. I Think, But Am Not Sure, that I had limited success with it in the game of trying to write a serious parody good enough to get published when I gave a copy to Philippa Foot. She read it and then engaged me on a couple of points so intensely that I felt obliged to say, "Philippa, you know this *is* a parody." Without missing a beat she rose to her full height and replied haughtily, "We *Do* Want To Get It *Right,* Don't We?"

Certainly not all the Oxford-Inspired Philosophers were disengaged from the political events of The 1960s as is often claimed. John Searle, visiting at Michigan, was intensely involved with The Free Speech Movement at his home university, Berkeley. He was appropriately working on Speech Acts at the time. After the strikes and speeches and marches and tear gassing and pepper gassing (I Was Gassed one day while having lunch at The Berkeley Faculty Club) and People's Park shootings were over, John took me on A Tour Of Campus Historic Sites. Now he says he does not remember this at all, but I am going to tell it the way I remember it

to illustrate the fact that Philosophers—like all Tellers Of Tales—
never let Getting Hung Up On The Facts keep them from Making
A Point.

We were loping across the campus—John has a long skier's
stride, even when Walking On The Grass—and John said, as I
recall, *something* like this: You know, Red, I always thought
Freudianism was bull, but here they are calling for revolution
and nobody was paying any attention, when this kid came on
campus with this sign that said FUCK, and the State Legislature
went ape—well, you know, I got to thinking maybe there is something to Freud after all.

Note again, John denies having said anything like that, although
I remember he did. But, as Descartes says, we are all prone to
error in the memory vein. Well, Each To His Own Speech Act.

Just as there are Hard-Headed Form-Oriented Ideal-Language
Techniques and Soft-Headed Content-Oriented Ordinary-Lan-
guage Gambits in Classic Analytic Philosophy, so are there also
the approaches of The Hard-Core Naturalist and The Soft-Core
Mystic to What It All Means. The hard-headed viewpoint of the
paper here titled "What *Does* It All Mean?" was in vogue in The
1970s. I suppose that it and "A Pig's Tail"—in which I show
How It All Unravels—come closest in this volume to expressing
My Own Viewpoint, to the extent that a comedian can be said
to have one. What I find amusing about this position is that when
you Take Off The Mask: Presto! There Is Nothing There. So
I do not have to write a before-my-time period piece on Atheistic
Sartrean Existentialism. Being-In-The-World is no more and no
less than giving things meaning. And without someone meaning
things, things wouldn't have meaning.

Ah, but came The Yearning 1980s. As we moved closer to
the last decade before The End of The Second Millennium, the
Yea-Sayers began coming out in droves like thousand-year locusts,
and by The Year 2000, the din will be deafening. The yearners
want mystical, transcendental intuition. There is even a Society

of (my italics) Christian Philosophers affiliated with The American Philosophical Association. All the other affiliated societies are not *of* but *for the study of.* But Never Mind. One of the brethren, a former colleague of mine, once whipped out a flier describing their journal and presented it to me with A Diabolical Christian Grin. He knew it would make me squirm, sort of the way a very straight heterosexual would if he saw a flier announcing that his old college roommate was coming out of the closet to be editor of a new gay magazine. But what is thoughtfully amusing about The Born-Lately Christians of The Reagan Era of American Philosophy is that some of the most stalwart of them made their reputations as Hard-Core Analysts, nay, even as Logical Positivists, whose crowning glory was to show that all that God Talk Is Nonsense. I should like to think that if my old colleague Charles L. Stevenson were now alive, he would not be a member of The Society. But I wouldn't bet on it.

The problem with Pascalian Wagerers is that they think The Choice is only between Atheism and The One True Religion. In the face of this Christian Revival, I find it soothing to look at The Absurd Theistic Existentialism of Kierkegaard. "The Seducer and the Seduced" is a little piece of Post-Modern Black Humor dedicated to my Washington University colleague Stanley Elkin. So we put Sex and Death together and what do we get? Dirty Words and Race Suicide.

A Man Grows Older; His Father Dies. I had The Good Fortune to be At My Father's Bedside during The Last Three Weeks Of His Life. Well, He Was An Old Man and You Have To Die Sometime. He would have lived longer if he had told someone sooner about the problem in his gut, but I think he figured The Hell With It. Or, more likely, Born In The Ozarks in 1900, he still believed with Back Country Wisdom that If You Go To the Hospital, You're Dead. Right. Afterwards I wrote "How to Die."

Old Friends sat in my father's hospital room Laughing and Telling Stories As He Lay Dying, he telling the most outrageous of them all. He was A Great Teller Of Tales, and it was, after all, *His* Deathbed Scene. The funniest episode, I thought, was when The Young Methodist Minister Came To Call. My father stopped attending The Methodist Church the day he retired as Superintendent of Schools in New Market, Iowa (pop. 350), many years before, so this preacher did not know him well, but you could see by the worried look on The Preacher's Face when he came on his Errand Of Mercy that he had heard tales. My father gave The Preacher a startled glance, rose up in bed on his bony elbows, pointed a trembling finger at the poor man, and whispered to me in a rasping voice audible up and down the entire hospital corridor, "Get That God Damned Fool Out Of Here!" Nevertheless, my father arranged to have A Masonic Funeral, like Harry Truman. One of the Songs He Wanted Sung was "School Days," but it was not deemed proper and, To My Eternal Shame, there was Not A God Damned Thing I Could Do About It.

Because my father's heart would not give out, it took him two weeks to die after he should have been dead. "Heart Like A Water Buffalo," The Doctor said.

"Why," My Brother Jim asked me as we were Jogging Along Together one day, "are we strengthening our hearts?"

Because What Man Can Do He Will, and he wants To Live Forever, or at least through next week, which comes to the same thing.

"Ape Dreams" is for The 1990s. Everything Goes. But how do you write about interbreeding humans and chimpanzees? I know too little about the biological details to write for Biologists. A straight paper in Ethics would be ludicrous; I mean, any serious piece on the subject would verge on self-parody, and I would not want that. It's not fun to be funny when you don't mean to. So finally I cast it in what I figured to be The Coming 1990s style. Borne Up By The Lightness Of Being In Cloud-Cuckoo Land, I blithely discuss the perfectly outrageous idea of screwing chimpanzees, in a breezy acceptance of every biotechnical possibility. Even so, I doubt that I have done justice to The Primal Sexual Urge. Everyone knows what King Kong wants when he abducts the Maiden, but ponder the following story: A small-time zoo keeper wants something that will really draw the crowds, so he decides to produce a Half-Breed by crossing A Female Gorilla with A Male Human Being. Of course he wants to do it in the cheapest, most obvious way, so he broaches the subject to his assistant, saying that it would be worth $400. His assistant says he will Think About It. Some three months later he comes into the zoo keeper's office and says he Will Do it.

"Why did you take so long to decide?" the Zoo Keeper asks.

His assistant replies, "You think it's easy to raise $400?"

Let me hasten, For The Record, to say that two Washington University Biologists, both women, have explained to me In Graphic Detail that because of pelvic and birth canal size, The Cross must be Male Ape and Female Human.

What *Does* It All Mean? The Relation of Truth of Content to Perfection of Form comes Full Circle in "A Pig's Tail." We Piss On Our Fathers' Graves to fertilize the trees growing from them. From trees we make paper. And on this paper we write our messages. And what do *they* all mean? I might say that they are contributions to The Conversation Richard Rorty calls for in lieu of Dead Serious Philosophy, although I do not actually understand why he is so Worked Up About Professional Philosophy. I know that he thinks it necessary to Do Philosophy In because it worships the wraith of The Absolute that escaped when We Killed God. It turns out, however, that Rorty is A Premature Optimist about the success of that operation. God's Legions On Earth still have Real Clout, but you can hardly say the same for most Philosophy Professors. Whatever. We still Give It The Old College Try.

I Come Onto The Stage with some sense of the absurdity of the entire enterprise, wearing A Paste-On Nose, Beating On Symbols, and dragging A Toy Duck On Wheels tied to My Shirt

Tail. I look out over The Blinding Footlights to The Unseen Audience, smile painfully, and hope I am Prepared To Meet The Menace.

A few years ago I read "The Seducer and the Seduced" at Emory University. After the talk a flustered woman came up to me and said, "How can you just *stand* there and *say* those things?" Aping my colleague, Bill Gass, I replied, "They're Just Words."

Contents

A Note From the Series Editor   5

Acknowledgments   7

Preface (After the Ball Is Over)   9

1. The Relation of Truth of Content to Perfection
    of Form in Literature (The 1950s)   21

2. Hopping and Skipping (The 1960s)   41

3. What *Does* It All Mean? (The 1970s)   55

4. The Seducer and the Seduced (The 1980s)   69

5. How to Die (The Pits)   89

6. Ape Dreams (The 1990s)   101

7. A Pig's Tail (The End of the Second Millennium) 117

1

The Relation of Truth of Content to Perfection of Form in Literature (The 1950s)

I. INTRODUCTION

Does the truth of the content of a work of literature have any necessary relation to the perfection of the form of that work? This paper makes intelligible how, according to an elementary realist theory of literature, one might come to a positive answer to this question. No claim is made that this conclusion is generalizable to all theories of literature; this paper shows only how this conclusion might be thought to follow from certain assumptions underlying the realist theory being considered. Given the explanation based on likeness which supports the relation of *representation* of fact by the content, and the relation of *carrying* of content by form, it is understandable how one might believe that there is a necessary relation between truth of content and perfection of form. It is concluded, however, that although the evidence makes it understandable how one might come to a positive answer, this answer is not conclusive, for the evidence does not rule out the logical possibility of denying that there is a necessary relation between truth of content and perfection of form.

II. THE TRUTH AS FACT AND TRUTH AS CORRESPONDENCE OF CONTENT TO FACT

Truth, in the grand sense, may simply be taken to be fact, or what is the case in the world. As facts are in the world, so would Truth be. It is assumed that such facts are easily enough known, and that the quest for Truth is a quest for knowledge of the world as it is. (The ambiguities of this usage should be obvious.) Suppose that it is this Truth of existent facts that a writer wishes to represent in literature. It might be said that such Truth is the content of his literary work.

However, this view of truth is inadequate in several ways. It is not accurate, for example, to say that *actual* facts are the content of literature. Rather, it is that the content of literature represents the facts. A correct representation of the facts by the content would allow one to call the content true to the facts, that is, true content. This is the sense of truth with which we shall be concerned, and it is undoubtedly appropriate to talk of the content of literature as being true in this sense.

This second sense of truth is employed in indicating the accuracy of representation by the content of the facts, that is, of Truth in the first sense. Hence, Truth *as* fact is not enough for characterizing the relation of content to fact. Truth as fact is also ambiguous, and may lead to confusions. Fortunately, it can be dispensed with entirely, for it is synonymous with the being or existence of the facts; rather than speak of Truth in the grand sense, one need merely speak of what has being or existence. This will cause no loss, for the grand sense of Truth has no opposing Falsehood, and hence is not useful as a mark of distinction. Anything which has being or exists would be said to have Truth, making it very hard to characterize Falsehood. The False, as opposed to the True, would be whatever does not have being or existence, which leads to problems we shall not consider here. For example, it seems to imply that *something* has the characteristic of Falseness, but if it must have being or existence to have a characteristic, such attribution leads to contradiction, for Falseness means non-being or non-existence.

The second sense of truth is more useful than the first, and it leads to no such paradoxes. Falsehood in opposition to such truth is easily characterized: content is false or untrue when it does not accurately represent or correspond to the facts. This is the notion of truth and falsity which is appealed to whenever a critic says of a work that it is not true to life. Accurate representation by content of fact, or correspondence of content to fact, then, is the sense of truth this paper employs. What is required to support the relation of representation has not yet, of course, been indicated here.

III. AN ELEMENTARY REALIST THEORY OF LITERATURE

With the above in mind, let us now consider an elementary realist theory of art. A work of art, the theory goes, should accurately represent life, nature, or the world, that is, the facts. A work of art should represent things as they are. For literature, this means at least that the content must be true to the facts. The question with which this paper is concerned is whether this implies anything about the form which carries the content.

To approach this question, consider the case of sculpture. The content of a piece of realistic statuary can be said to represent some fact in the world. Suppose the statue represents the shape of a certain man. Then to represent truly the shape of this man, the content of the statue must be an accurate representation of his shape. The artist accomplishes this by reproducing the man's shape; the content of the statue truly represents the man's shape by being an exact copy of it. And in this case, this means that the form of the statue must duplicate the shape of the man in order for the content of the statue to be true. Form and content of the statue are necessarily coextensive. The relation of representation here rests upon the point-by-point correspondence or resemblance of form and content with the shape represented.

IV. DOES THE FORM OF LITERATURE NECESSARILY CHANGE WITH ITS CONTENT?

A. Fact, Content, Matter, and Form in Literature

Let us now return to literature. Is there any relation—necessary or otherwise—between the content of literature and the form of literature as there is in the case of the realistic statue? Does the form of literature necessarily change with the truth or falsity of the content as it does in the statue? This implies a more general question which we shall consider first: Does the form of literature necessarily change with its content? If this question is answered positively, then we can consider whether this correspondence is dependent upon the truth of the content.

Offhand, the answer to the general question would seem to be no. Considerations which are hard to grasp, or which are relative, or at least about which there is no common agreement, such as tone, mood, and so on, still seem to provide a solid basis for answering this question negatively. It would be claimed that an accurate literary representation can be given of the same fact in two very different ways, that is, the same true content can be carried in literature by two (or more) different forms. One of these forms might have perfection, the other not. And even though we have not yet considered just what perfection of form is, examples seem numerous. No argument seems necessary.

But is this really the case? *Can* two different forms equally well carry the same content? Consider again the example of the realistic statue. The correspondence of the content and form of the statue to the fact is one of likeness, of imitation, similarity, duplication, reproduction, imagery, or of picturing. It seems obvious that literature cannot picture fact in any strict literal sense. Where would this picture be found? We have so far discussed the *fact* represented, the *content* which represents, and the *form* which carries this content. There is also the *matter* which in literature consists of words—written or spoken and arranged in various ways—which represent the form and carry the content. In the case of the statue, the matter would be stone or some other material; the matter of the statue is three-dimensional just as is the shape represented, so it does not hinder form and content from duplicating that shape. But what seems obvious on an elementary level with literature is that neither the matter nor the form of literature is similar to the content each carries, nor are matter and form similar to the fact this content represents. However, the realist theory under consideration requires a similarity between fact, content, matter, and form in literature; it is part of the purpose of this paper to make intelligible one kind of similarity which could pertain among these elements.

B. The Relations of Representing and Carrying Based on Likeness

This paper has no intention of examining just what the content of literature *is,* other than saying that it represents facts. The concern here is merely with the relations of *representation* and of *carrying* in the realist theory under consideration. In this theory it is assumed that the truth of the content depends upon its exact correspondence with the facts. It is further implied that this correspondence is likeness of some sort. In some sense content represents fact truly because it gives an accurate picture of it. We can accept this requirement without inquiring into *what* the content is (in the sense that we know what the matter is, i.e., words), because it will be seen that the explication of the sense of likeness required between content and fact does not depend upon knowing what the content is.

Suppose we agree that content represents fact because there is a likeness or resemblance in some sense between them. This likeness explains how content can be of fact, that is, it can represent fact because it resembles it; content pictures (in some sense) fact. Once this is accepted, one might accept a similar answer to the question of how form can carry content. If one accepts as unproblematic the notion that content *represents* fact because of the relation of likeness between the two, then one might thereby be led to accept as plausible the contention that form can *carry* content because of likeness between form and content. A futher consideration drawing one to this conclusion is the fact that the matter (words) both *represents* form and *carries* content, and could be said to be able to do both of these tasks because of the mutual likeness (in some sense) of the matter to both form and content.

This certainly seems to be one plausible way of talking about fact, content, matter, and form in the case of a realistic statue. Content represents fact, matter carries content and represents form, form carries content—all because of mutual likeness among the four elements. Incidently, this gives us an answer to the general question: Does the form of realistic sculpture necessarily change with its content? The answer, obviously, is yes. The answer to the more specific question of whether form necessarily changes with truth of content in realistic sculpture would also seem to be yes. For the truth of content is dependent upon accurate representation by content of fact; and since the relation of representation rests on that of likeness, any change in fact would necessarily be reflected in the content which is true of it. Content and form are coextensive here, so this means that any change in content calculated to keep that content true to the fact it represents would necessitate a change in form. Every content, then, would be carried by a unique form; no two contents could be carried by the same form, nor could two forms carry the same content, for where there is a difference in one there is necessarily a corresponding—like—difference in the other.

On the other hand, the matter of sculpture, it might be contended, is not so uniquely determined. Whether this is so will be considered later; now it is enough to remark that the matter of sculpture, wood or stone or whatever, is still like fact, content, and form in being three-dimensional.

C. For Each Content in Literature is There a Unique Form Best Fitted to Carry It?

Is it the case in literature that all forms differ one from another by being uniquely fitted to carry one and only one content? Each content, of course, is uniquely fitted to be true of one and only one fact (both content and fact could be complex). True representation depends upon the point-by-point correspondence of fact by content. Is such correspondence or likeness necessary between the form and the content it carries? Let us approach this question by considering the matter of literature. If we consider words in their relations of representing form and carrying content, we seem at first to find evidence that likeness or resemblance is not necessary. For after all, it is claimed, spoken and written words of many different languages can equally adequately represent the same form and carry the same content. (Note that the contention that different matters can represent the same form and carry the same content is presented here as a claim; the truth of this claim will be considered later.) Sounds and orthography of different languages differ; consequently we would be wrong, it might be claimed, to say that likeness is necessary between the matter and either the content it carries or the form it represents.

Concluding that likeness is not necessary between matter and content for matter to *carry* content, one might argue that since *carrying* can occur without likeness between the elements, form could *carry* content without being like it. It might even be argued that since likeness is not necessary between matter and form for matter to *represent* form, one could wonder if it is really necessary for there to be likeness between content and fact for content to *represent* fact.

These arguments lead to a challenge of the contention that for every particular content in literature, there is necessarily a unique form which can best carry it. If form carries content because of likeness between them, then uniqueness is implied. The opposition is based on the seeming fact that different matters can equally well carry the same content and represent the same form. If matter need not be like what it carries, why should form? Without the necessity for likeness, the argument for uniqueness is said to collapse. We shall postpone for a moment the question of whether matter *can* carry content and represent form without being like them.

Let us first note that a positive answer to the question of whether each content in literature is necessarily related to a unique form might be indicated by general agreement that certain *kinds* of form seem more appropriate for carrying certain *kinds* of content than do other kinds of form. Some kinds of form are more appropriate to funeral dirges, for example, than others. If this is true, and it is agreed that particular contents of the same kind still differ among themselves, and that particular forms of the same kind also differ among themselves, then it might be expected that there is a unique form of a certain kind for every unique content of a certain kind. This might be the case even if form carried content without likeness between them. Just because it follows that if different forms can carry the same content, then the carrying relation cannot rest on exact likeness between form and content, it does *not* follow that if there is no likeness between form and content, then different forms can carry the same content. Uniqueness of form to content may still pertain. Hence, even if it were true that matter carries content and represents form; and form carries content *without* likeness between matter, content, and form; this would still not be enough to show that there is not a unique form best fitted to each content.

Further, even if the same form could be represented by different matters, and the same content could be carried by different matters, there is no assurance that this is the same sort of *carrying* as pertains between form and content, nor the same sort of *representation* as pertains between content and fact. Uniqueness may be unnecessary for matter to carry and represent, but necessary for form to carry and/or content to represent. Such is the case in the example of the statue where it is assumed (*though not proved*) that matter could change without altering form or content.

To deny that there is a unique form best fitted to carry each content in literature, then, one must show explicitly that two forms can carry the same content. It is not enough to show (nor has it been shown) that likeness is not required to support this carrying. If it can be shown that different forms *can* carry the same content (even while admitting that content represents fact because of likeness between content and fact), then, of course, this is enough to show that the carrying relation does not rest on likeness between form and content.

The overall purpose of this paper is to give one possible interpretation of the elementary realist theory of literature stated earlier. According to this interpretation, we shall see that if one assumes that form does not carry content because of likeness between them, or that matter needs no likeness to form and content, then one cannot intelligibly assume that content represents fact because it has a likeness to fact; or, conversely, that if one assumes that content represents fact because of likeness between them, then one cannot intelligibly assume that matter need not be like form and content, nor that the relation of carrying of content by form rests on anything other than likeness between content and form. Though there is no logical impossibility here, once the explanatory force of likeness between fact and content is used to explain how content represents fact, then it is most comprehensible to base also in likeness between the elements the relations of matter carrying content, matter representing form, and form carrying content. If all explanations of representation and carrying are based on likeness between fact, content, matter, and form, then it follows that there is a unique content best fitted to represent each fact, a unique matter best fitted to represent each form and carry each content, and, finally, a unique literary form best fitted to carry each literary content. Consequently, to answer the title question of this section, the form of literature does—according to this interpretation— necessarily change with its content.

V. IS FORM LIKE FACT?

The picture drawn now is one in which likeness between the world and the content gives explanatory support to the relation of representation between them, likeness between the matter (words) and the content gives explanatory support to the relation of carrying between them, likeness between matter and form gives explanatory support to the relations of representation between them, and likeness between form and content gives explanatory support to the relation of carrying between them. The implication here seems to be that form is like fact. It may be thought that this need not necessarily follow: the likeness between fact and content, for example, could be based on a different aspect of content than that aspect which is like form; it could even be the case that the content is different from fact just to the extent that it is like the form. But the development of the theory certainly seems to lead one to believe that it is implied that form is like fact. If one considers that the relation between content and fact is one of correspondence (and correspondence means likeness), then it would seem to be the case that to whatever extent the content were unlike the fact, to that extent it would not correspond to it, that is, it would not be true to it. A content which truly represented a fact would necessarily have to correspond to it completely, it seems. And in such case there would be no aspect of the true content which *could* be different from the fact in the sense of not being like it. So if there is any likeness between content and form, it would seem to have to be based on the same aspects in which the content is like fact. Consequently, it seems to follow that if content represents fact because it is like it, and form carries content because of likeness between them, then form is like fact.

VI. WHAT SENSE OF LIKENESS IS REQUIRED?

Still, it seems to be obvious that matter and form in literature cannot be like fact and content in the sense of being pictures or copies of them. Onomatopoeia may suggest an exception, but the fact that some words sound like the things they represent (or like the carried content which represents the things), and the fact that some martial poetry on the printed page and in its sound carries with it a resemblance to certain aspects of marching platoons might seem to be accidental. But is this resemblance really accidental? Can it not be said that love poetry written in certain meters simply does not accurately represent the facts, not because the content is not true to the facts, but because the form is inappropriate for carrying the content? Such form would be said to be not true to (unlike) the (content or the) facts.

Some explanatory basis for contending that certain forms are not appropriate to certain contents or facts might be found if it could be explained how literary form is like content or fact. An untrue form would then be unlike the content it carries, just as an untrue content is unlike the fact it represents.

To discover what sort of likeness might pertain between form and content or fact, let us first examine the nature of facts. They have a structure to the extent that they contain elements which are distributed in space and/or time. Suppose we consider as such just this pattern in space and/or time, not considering what the facts or their elements *are* which exist in space and/or time. Now, though this paper does not give an explanation of just what content as such *is,* let us consider content. Without knowing what it *is,* we know that it must have a structure, since it is a content which, in the elementary realist theory, represents facts which are in space and/or time by being like them. It has, then, a pattern or structure which can be considered as such, without any concern either with what the content is or with what the content as a whole represents. This provides us with a notion of likeness— that of isomorphism of structure—which can pertain between fact and content, whether or not the likeness between them is exact resemblance as it is in the case of the realistic statue. In explicating this notion of structural isomorphism we have indicated the structural elements of spatial and/or temporal pattern, but of course similarity of any other structural elements in fact and content would do as well.

VII. DOES LITERARY MATTER AND FORM HAVE A STRUCTURE ISOMORPHIC WITH THAT OF FACT AND CONTENT?

Now we must examine literary form to see if it also has a structure which could possibly be like that of content, thus providing an explanatory basis to support the carrying of content by form. Literary form is not represented simply by the shape and sound of words and sequences of them, but also by the entire representation of the literary work. Among other things, this includes blocks of slow passages, swift passages, staccato passages, stumbling passages; it includes the sound of passages when read; and it includes the overall weight of the work. This *matter* of sound and geometric design has a structure deriving from its distribution in space and/or time. Not only can one consider this structure apart from the matter which carries it, one can plausibly contend that the structural pattern indicated just *is* the literary form carried by the matter. Literary form, then, would be nothing more than the structure of the matter of literature, which structure can be abstracted from that matter as the matter exists in space and/or time. And if there is any likeness, or any need of likeness, between fact and content, and between written or spoken word (the matter) and literary form, then the most likely candidate for this likeness is the structure which is common to them all. Not pictorial likeness, then, but rather isomorphism of structural patterns resulting from their mutual existence in space and/or time would be the relation of likeness which necessarily pertains among form, matter, content, and fact in literature. In the elementary realist theory under consideration, the existence of such structural likeness is a strong inducement for employing it to explain not only the required (because assumed in order to explain the representation) likeness between content and fact, but also to explain how matter can carry content and represent form, and how form can carry matter. As we have seen, such a theory would imply that there is a unique form fit for each particular content, and a unique matter fit for each form and each content.

VIII. HESITATIONS ABOUT THE MATTER

But is there a unique literary matter for each form and each content? If it is to be contended that the same form can be represented in different languages, and that the same content can be carried by different languages, then it might be claimed that there is no unique matter for each content and form. Consider the matter of a statue. Will it be wood or stone? They are equally capable of duplicating the shape of the model. Similarly, the argument would run, any literary matter is adequate for representing form and carrying content.

This last conclusion is probably not true. Some forms and some contents evidently cannot be represented in all languages, for the structural possibilities differ in different languages, just as wood and stone do differ in their capacities for representing shapes. And though it might seem generally to be true that interchangeability without disrupting form and content is possible between languages of the same family, even this can be challenged. Surely the matter of French is better fitted for carrying some contents and representing some forms than is the matter of English, and vice versa. But the point need not be argued by giving examples. If the principles of structural likeness are employed for explaining the relations of carrying and representing, it can be concluded that for every fact there is a unique content, a unique matter (words in a specific language), and a unique literary form, all necessarily related because each has the same structure.

IX. DOES THE FORM OF LITERATURE NECESSARILY CHANGE WITH CONTENT?

The answer to the general question raised early in this paper, "Does the form of literature necessarily change with its content?" can now be given. Form does necessarily change with content if the following is assumed:

1. The purpose of literature is to represent reality.

2. Likeness is required between any two elements, one of which either (a) represents the other, or (b) carries the other. (These two relations might be combined as the relation of exhibiting.)

3. Such likeness pertains in the aspect of structural isomorphism among fact, content which represents fact, matter which carries content and represents form, and form which carries content. This likeness of structure extends through fact, content, matter, and form because each of them has a pattern dependent upon its existence in space and/or time. Indeed, it follows from this theory that literary form is identical with this abstracted structural pattern.

Obviously, then, wherever content changes to fit fact, form must necessarily change to fit content if literature is to maintain its true representation of reality.

X. DOES THE FORM OF LITERATURE NECESSARILY CHANGE WITH TRUTH OF CONTENT?

Our more specific question is whether literary form necessarily changes with the truth of content. Obviously it does, for the theory demands true representation.

XI. IS THERE A RELATION BETWEEN TRUE CONTENT AND PERFECTION OF FORM?

Having given these answers—at least for the realist theory under consideration, and note that this paper does not advocate it, but merely shows one way of interpreting it that makes it both under-standable and plausible—we can go on now to consider the relation, if any, between true content and perfection of form. If perfection of form merely indicates the unique adequateness of each form for carrying a particular true content, then of course any form which carries a true content adequately is perfect. Any work of literature representing false content would necessarily have an imperfect form. This conclusion follows necessarily from the interpretation given of the realist theory under consideration.

Further support for this conclusion might be provided by argument to show that the True and the Beautiful are really the same. We shall not analyze these arguments, but will only say that while the explanation suggested herein of a possible necessary relation between form and true content seems plausible, it does not seem to follow from this explanation alone that the unique form necessarily related to each true content is thereby an *aesthetically* perfect form, though it might be the perfect form for carrying that particular true content. That is, a criterion of *aesthetic* perfection in form is required, but it does not seem obvious that aesthetic perfection of form is equivalent to perfection pertaining because a form is uniquely fitted to carry (and/or is carrying) some true content. Even supposing that there were no problems in determining whether content is true, and that matter and form are appropriate; and even assuming that in every known case forms carrying true contents are aesthetically perfect while forms carrying false contents are not; if aesthetic perfection is not *equated* to perfection in function, then this coincidence would still not be enough to show that true content is necessarily related to aesthetically perfect form. One might assert that the criterion for aesthetic perfection in form is the form's perfect functioning in carrying content, but this paper has so far uncovered nothing which would allow one to prove the assertion.

If one accepted perfect in function as the criterion of aesthetic perfection, it might seem that the same form would have aesthetic perfection when carrying true content, and aesthetic *im*perfection when carrying false content. This would imply that a form has aesthetic perfection only in relation to true content (and also to fact and adequate matter), whether causally or contextually. But are there not some forms which are more adequately fitted than others for carrying false contents? A false content is merely a content which inadequately represents fact. But any form which adequately carries that false content perfectly must (according to the theory) surely have to be isomorphic with it in structure. Perhaps we need to specify the criterion to state that aesthetic perfection pertains to any form which perfectly carries its content, whether that content be true or false. For surely some forms which carry false content have aesthetic perfection; the more specific criterion explains why. One could then extend the analogy between the way content represents fact and the way form carries content. A false content is one which inadequately represents a fact; an imperfect form is one which inadequately carries a content, whether the content is true or false. Even here, however, it is not obvious that such imperfection of form in carrying out its function is equivalent to aesthetic imperfection. It is neither obvious that aesthetic perfection resides in a form as such, nor that it pertains to a form when it is functioning adequately.

But one might very well be led on whatever grounds—perhaps by a higher criterion of simplicity, or symmetry—to conclude that perfection in function of form is either identical to, or the criterion of, aesthetic perfection. Then it would be contended, in the strongest sense, that aesthetic perfection pertains to form *only* in a context where fact, content, matter, and form all have the same structure, that is, only when literature represents the world as it really is. There would be, then, a necessary relation between true content and perfection of form.

If anyone should disagree with this criterion—and there are those who do—argument either stops, or another criterion of aesthetic perfection must be exhibited for examination. It might be contended in objection, for example, that aesthetic perfection is in none of the four elements here mentioned, nor in the relations among them, but is merely a term of approbation used by an observer. Or it might be agreed that aesthetic perfection is dependent upon the context, but that we have failed to delineate the context completely since we left out (or at least did not explicitly include) the artist and/or the observer and/or their respective roles. For example, we have said nothing about the selection of content (or of fact to be represented) by the artist. The theory presented implies that whatever *is* is beautiful, at least in the sense of having a structure isomorphic with a perfect form. But it might be claimed that the essence of artistic representation rests in selection, which might lead to contentions that the artist either creates a work of art which is truer than life, or which falsifies the facts.

XII. CONCLUSION

But these last are possibilities and problems we shall not pursue further. Our aim here has been merely to consider an elementary realist theory of literature in order to exhibit its underlying principles, which are that the relations of representation and carrying depend upon likeness between the elements, and to make this theory understandable by giving one plausible interpretation of what the required likeness might be, i.e., structural similarity abstracted from fact, content, matter, and form which are all existent in space and/or time. In following out the implications of such an interpretation, this paper concludes that there is a necessary relation in this theory between true content and form, but it is left to the reader's judgment whether to conclude that *functional perfection* of form in carrying true content is or is not equivalent to the criterion of *aesthetic perfection* of form.

XIII. POSTSCRIPT

However, this analysis does suggest that whoever says that Truth is Beauty, or that Beauty is Truth, may be able to make his statements intelligible only with the explication given above. That is, if truth amounts to correspondence between what represents and what is represented, and this with the maxim that Truth is Beauty is taken to imply a realistic theory of art, then it seems plausible to suppose that this correspondence is based in—that the representation amounts to—likeness, similarity, or resemblance between the representation and what is represented. In fact, such resemblance between representation and its object is one of the most obvious features of realistic art. Thus, one might claim, the closer the representation comes to resembling exactly the object represented, the truer is this representation, and also the more beautiful.

The most beautiful (perfection) would be that which exactly re-sembles the model—and this could lead to what might be thought to be an absurd conclusion, i.e., that the model itself is its own most beautiful representation.

Perhaps we have reached a *reductio*. It might plausibly be contended that every thing resembles every thing to some extent, and therefore that any thing can represent (if resemblance is neces-sary to representation) any thing. This would be true *if* every thing *were* like every other thing in just one respect. We shall not go into that question.[1] But it is true upon the explication given that the *degree* of resemblance must be specified. And if beauty is dependent only upon degree of accuracy in representation, then one can hardly avoid concluding that the most perfect art object is the model itself. Some other criterion is necessary (e.g., economy, simplicity, balance) besides accuracy of representation if this absurd-ity is to be avoided. This seems to be enough to conclude not only that the elementary realistic theory (with what surely is the most plausible interpretation one can give of it) is inadequate, but also that any realistic theory of art is inadequate to the extent that the criterion of aesthetic perfection is taken to be realistic representation.

---

1. On degrees of likeness: It might even be the case that ubiquitous likeness in our world is the main reason it is understandable (for it allows comparisons and generalizations), and the reason that any one thing can represent another at all. Two natural languages, it might be claimed, obviously have the same structure to some degree in being about the same world. This would not decide the question of whether one language is better fitted to express a certain content than another language, but it does point up the difficulty of deciding which structural features are important.

2

Hopping and Skipping[1]
(The 1960s)

I. INTRODUCTION

When would we say, "He is hopping", and when would we say, "He is skipping"?

---

1. I should like to acknowledge the assistance in writing this paper given to me by the assistant parts manager (whose name unfortunately I do not know) of the Volkswagen garage in Ann Arbor, Michigan, particularly for consultation in the difficult task of describing skipping, and I should like to thank Jacqueline F. Austin, housewife and commercial cave operator, Horse Cave, Kentucky, for a critical reading she gave this paper, even though she disagrees violently with several points herein.

II. HOPPING

When we say that a man is hopping we imply two things: First, that he intends to engage in a certain sort of overt physical activity, and second, that he exhibits that activity by his behavior. The first is the more important. This intention is a mental action, although we imply thereby neither that there are minds nor mental acts.

What is a man's intention when he intends to hop? Let us examine some ordinary things we might say about a man with such an intention:

1. "Here is a man who just joined in a children's game, 'Hop, Skip, and Jump'.[2] As a matter of course he will abide by the rules of the game."

2. "Here is a man who has just been told by his physician— who wishes to check his blood pressure—to hop up and down on one foot fifty times. It is part of the physician's regular routine to ask his patients to follow this set procedure, and this man always does what his physician tells him to do."

3. "Here is a man who has just bet his small son fifty cents that he (the father) can hop a distance of one block. The son is watching for him to start, and will be sure to catch any infraction in the rules of hopping."

4. "Here is a man who must proceed, but finds a puddle in his way. He has just remarked to a bystander that he is going to hop over it. If he does this incorrectly, he may fall in."

---

2. Jumping is an involved subject. I intend to take it up in another and much longer article.

In each of these cases it is implied either that hopping involves certain rules of behavior or that there are right and wrong ways of hopping. Hopping, then, obviously is an achievement at which one can have success. The intention to hop, then, in its ordinary sense includes the intention to hop according to the rules, or rightly. (One could, of course, intend to hop in such a fashion as to break the rules, or wrongly. We would then say, "You are not hopping according to the rules", or "You are hopping wrongly". In the first case, one might be hopping *rightly,* but not according to the rules of a game or activity which includes hopping. In the second case, one might hop wrongly to various degrees, until at some unspecified point we might say to him, "You are not *hopping at all!*") What one intends to do, then, when one intends to hop, is to behave in a certain specified manner.

From this examination of what we would say about a man who is intending to hop, we have discovered that hopping is a rule-governed activity. What else can we learn about hopping from our examples? From (1) and (4) it is implied that a certain skill is required for hopping, otherwise it would not be included as part of a game, nor would the ordinary man pause before doing it. People sometimes make games of walking, but only the abnormal pause before attempting it.[3,4]

---

3. Of course there are walking contests, and "walking" is one of the events engaged in by participants at track meets. But this is a *technical* use of the term 'walking'; track-meet walking is so defined that the heel of the forward foot must touch the ground before the toe of the rear foot is permitted to leave the ground. In doing this participants waggle their hips in a way that observers always find to be hilarious and slightly obscene. This is certainly not the ordinary way of walking. On the subject of walking, it might be remarked that hopping and skipping *could* be considered as aberrant forms of walking (ordinary sense). That this is not obviously so will be apparent to most readers upon a moment's reflection.

4. One might say that the use of 'hop' in the name of the game "Hop, Skip, and Jump" is also a technical sense. It is not, and the difference is that "Hop, Skip, and Jump" *as children play it* is not a formal game, while track-

From (2) one learns that hopping can be done on one foot, and that it is done up and down. However, in (3) we discover that one can also hop a horizontal distance, supposedly in a series of hops, although in (4) it surely is the case that the puddle is to be cleared in one movement.

From these examples, then, we cannot determine the exact definition of the activity of hopping. The major difficulties come from (2) where the specific instructions seem to suggest the possibility that one might hop on more or less than one leg, and that hopping can involve horizontal movement instead of, or as well as, up and down. The second possibility is immediately set forth in (3) and (4). This leaves us some perplexity.

My presentation is calculated to bring this result.

"But surely," we would say, "we all know what hopping is. Hopping is the propelling of the body off the ground up and down with one leg while the other leg is held off the ground. It can be done with either leg, and can be done while staying in the same place (i.e., always leaving from and landing on the same spot), or a horizontal component can be put into the propellent force, so the body is not only propelled upward, but also along horizontally (in any horizontal direction). One can hop along, then, as well as up and down, hopping up from one spot to move along horizontally to come down on another spot. Thus, hopping is a form of vertical, or combined vertical and horizontal, loco-motion."

But *does* one *really* (know what hopping is)?

Two senses of hopping (ordinary) have already been distinguished, or perhaps better, one sense and a variation. It might be said that hopping *simpliciter* is just hopping up and down. Hopping along would be a compound of hoppings *simpliciter*. There are difficulties with this which we shall examine immediately.

---

meet walking is. As a matter of fact, there is an event in track meets called the "Hop, Skip, and Jump", but surely we need not consider that here.

Would we say, "I am hopping rope"? Yet, one can *skip* rope by propelling one's body up and down with (on) one leg, leaving and landing always in the same spot.[5] The same sort of objection can be made to the claim that hopping along is the basic form of hopping. One can skip rope on one leg, always leaving from one spot and landing in another.

Perhaps the "essence" of hopping is passing over something.[6] This is suggested by example (4) in which a man passes over a puddle by hopping over it. Yet, metaphorical usage (always suggestive of the non-metaphorical usage from which it is derived) seems to deny this. We would never say when reading a book that we are hopping a paragraph here and there; rather, we would say, "I am *skipping* a paragraph here and there". Nor do we ever say, "Hop it", when we mean for someone to pass over something; we say, "Skip it".[7]

And *is* hopping restricted to propelling the body with one leg? How would one describe the forward movement of a man who had both legs tied in a potato sack? Surely we would say, "He is hopping along".[8] And what about horses? Surely a horse, to be said to be hopping, need not propel himself with one leg. A horse hops on two legs (his hind ones),[9] and might very well

---

5. My specific point of disagreement with Mrs. Austin is over this matter of skipping rope. Mrs. Austin insists that one does not skip rope, but that one *jumps* rope. I cannot go into this matter now, so you must take my word for it that she is wrong. (As indicated above, Mrs. Austin's home state is Kentucky.)

6. What will be shown is that it is improper to look for a common element in hopping at all.

7. This will cause difficulties when we consider skipping.

8. Admittedly this may be a technical use.

9. If a horse "hopped" on his two front legs, would we call it hopping? I do not believe a horse can do this. But a man (an acrobat) can stand on his hands and can move along by propelling himself up and down along on his hands. My sensitivity to language use, however, suggests to me that it would be going too far to call this hopping.

hop on four (whether or not tied together in a potato sack). There does, however, seem to be a restriction in the other direction. A millipede might hop, but a man with no legs could not.[10,11]

What about the horizontal component in hopping? Could it be the essence of hopping? Suppose my wife tells me to hop down to the store to get something for supper (or to hop up and answer the door). Surely she does not mean for me to go on one leg. But she does mean for me to move horizontally to the store or door. So hopping sometimes involves nothing more than moving horizontally. Sometimes 'hop' is even a transitive verb. One can hop onto something, and vagrants often hop freights, meaning not that they pass over them, but that they catch onto them and swing[12] aboard.

Finally, one must, of course, be careful in attempting to gain insight into hopping by examining the use of 'hop' as a noun or a name. For example, at the "Sophomore Hop" one finds dancing, as in the "Lindy Hop", not hopping. But there is some significance in some names. "Hopalong" as in "Hopalong Cassidy", may have some reference to the way the man mounts his horse. (Later we shall see that perhaps Cassidy would have been better named "Skipalong".) "Hoppy" might be short for "Hopalong", or else it might be a child's name for a pet rabbit; "Hopper" would do as well. (Note that rabbits have never been known to hop on one leg. Nor have kangaroos.) "Hop-head", of course, sometimes has no reference to hopping at all, although hop-heads sometimes get hopping mad.

Before passing on (hopping?) to a consideration of skipping—

---

10. But see note 8.

11. Yet, things without legs do hop. As airplane dispatchers we might say, "TW47 took a short hop to Bermuda yesterday". But when we say, "The joint is hopping tonight", we do not mean that something without legs is hopping, but only that the people with legs in it are, although even that is not clear.

12. A consideration of swinging would take us too far afield.

without which we can come to no definitive conclusions concerning hopping—we shall answer the following question: Can a man be said to be hopping if he is not intending to, but is only exhibiting the overt behavior of the sort described in this section? The answer, categorically, is no. Hopping, as we are considering it, is a combination of intentional activity and motion. We would not say that a man who only intends to hop is hopping. And a man who exhibits movement that he does not intend[13] to exhibit might have a nervous disease, e.g., "the hops", but we would not say that he is *hopping*.

III. SKIPPING

When we say that a man is skipping we imply, as in the case of hopping, that he intends to engage in a certain sort of overt physical activity, and that he exhibits that activity by his behavior. We can examine a man's intention when he intends to skip by considering some ordinary things we might say about him:

1. "Here is a man who has just joined in a children's game, 'Hop, Skip, and Jump'.[14] As a matter of course he will abide by the rules of the game."

2. "Here is a man who has just been told by his physician— who wishes to check his blood pressure—to skip around the room three times. It is part of the physician's regular routine to ask his patients to follow this set procedure,

---

13. This is a strong statement, illustrative of a weaker thesis. That is, further investigation would show that one very well might *hop* without intending to. The weaker thesis is that hopping is merely movement and not also intentional activity.

14. See footnotes 2–4, *mutatis mutandis*.

and this man always does what his physician tells him to do."

3. "Here is a man who has just bet his small son fifty cents that he (the father) can skip a distance of one block. The son is watching for him to start, and will be sure to catch any infractions in the rules of skipping."

4. "Here is a man who must proceed, but finds a group of merry revel-makers in his way. He has just remarked to a bystander that he is going to proceed by skipping, thereby passing through the revel-makers by joining in with them. If he does it poorly, they will surely discern his serious purpose and detain him."

As in the hopping examples, these cases show that the intention is to skip according to the rules, or rightly. (If one skipped very poorly, we might say, "You're not *skipping* at all!") Skipping, also, obviously is an achievement at which one can have success. What one intends to do, then, when one intends to skip, is to behave in a certain specified manner.

Skipping is also a rule-governed activity. It involves skills, but they are ordinary skills.[15] There is no hint, however, in these examples as to how skipping is done. It does seem clear from examples (2)–(4) that one can move along horizontally by skipping. Let us see what help our ordinary knowledge of what skipping is will give us.[16] We would say: "Skipping is moving one leg

---

15. I believe there *is* a set of formalized rules for skipping rope in which 'skipping' has a technical definition. These rules might be invoked, e.g., by fraternity boys trying to set the world's record for number of consecutive rope skips. Our concern, however, is with the ordinary sense of skipping which is involved in the informal children's activity of skipping rope. See also footnotes 3 and 4, *mutatis mutandis*.

16. Of course this is quite legitimate, even necessary, procedure. In any analysis of the concepts, use, or usage of ordinary language, we use what we

forward and placing the foot attached to it on the ground; then, while the other leg is being moved forward and is still in the air, propelling one's body upward off the ground with the first leg, landing on the foot attached to that first leg before placing the second foot (which is attached to the other leg and which has been moving forward off the ground all this time and is now in front of the first foot) on the ground. The vertical motion of the body is then initiated by the leg to which that second foot is attached while the first leg moves forward through the air again. The movement is repeated in sequence, first with one leg, and then with the other. The vertical propulsion can be executed *simpliciter,* i.e., leaving from and landing on the same spot, or it can contain a horizontal component so that the foot leaves from one spot and lands on another. Thus, skipping is a form of locomotion which combines vertical and horizontal components."

An immediate conclusion seems to follow, giving us a distinction between hopping and skipping. Hopping can include merely a vertical component, or combine a horizontal with that vertical component; skipping, on the other hand, necessarily is a combination of vertical and horizontal components. One can hop in one place, but one cannot skip in one place.

Yet, we do say that people often do just that—skip in one place—when they are skipping rope.

Hence, it just will not do for us to say that a common element in skipping is horizontal motion. Could it be that the common element in skipping is the leaving from and landing on the ground of one foot while the other foot is not toucing the ground? This will not do either, for it is as much an element of certain kinds of hopping. (Indeed, in urgent situations, a person may hop from one foot to the other.) In fact, what should be obvious by now is that *skipping* includes one *variant* of hopping. Skipping is one

---

ordinarily—common-sensically—know, both as a starting point and as a check for our analyses.

possible combination of walking and hopping.[17] Consequently, it should not now be perplexing as to why we say we *skip* rope rather than *hop* rope. The close relation of the terms has led to confusion in usage. This confusion extends to metaphorical usage. Obviously, it would be more accurate[18] if we were to say that we hopped over certain paragraphs rather than skipped over them in reading. And certainly "Hop it!" is more graphic than "Skip it!"

What other uses do we have for 'skipping'? A horse can skip (a circus horse) much as a man does, although the description of this feat would take more space than we can spare here. (Think of a millepede!) Things without legs can also skip. My typewriter skips spaces, and flat rocks can be sent skipping across a surface of water. (Would it not be better to say that typewriters and rocks hop?) We do not say that joints are skipping, although surely that would convey a more merry tone than to say that they are hopping. 'Skipping', like 'hopping', also may indicate only the component of horizontal motion. We say that some people skip the country, meaning neither that they skip through it or over it, but that they move out of it. Students skip classes (although they could equally be said to hop over them). And there is also a transitive element when we say that someone skipped out on his wife.

As for 'skip' as a noun or a name, it no doubt is (or will

---

17. The dictionary defines skipping as "a step and a hop". This is obviously inadequate, because it does not really move one along. I take up stepping in my work on ordinary walking (in progress); there is not space enough to get into it deeply here. But consider: 'Stepping' has no ordinary use in the sense of moving along, although it does imply this in metaphorical and technical uses as in "stepping out" and "goose-stepping". We would find it odd, however, to say, "He is stepping downtown", when we mean "He is walking downtown". (There are problems with this last, too, of course.) I have found it best not to use these misleading terms—'step' and 'stepping'—in this short paper.

18. In a very literal sense, of course.

be) used for a dance called "The Skip."[19] Small boys and dogs are sometimes called "Skippy", which may or may not be descriptive of some aspects of their behavior.[20] And recalling the Cassidy movies of my youth, it does seem to me that "Skipalong Cassidy" would be more graphic than "Hopalong", for he often does skip just before mounting his horse. But, of course, there is an overlap here, and I am not suggesting that names should be descriptive.[21] "Skipper", of course, when used in referring to the captain of a ship, has no reference to skipping at all.[22]

Before comparing our findings about hopping and skipping, we can answer a question concerning skipping similar to that which we asked about hopping. Can a man be said to be skipping if he is not intending to, but is only exhibiting overt behavior of the sort described in this section? No. Skipping also is a combination of action and activity. A man who only intends to skip is not skipping. And a man might behave in a certain way because he has "the skips" (a disease), but, unless he intended to,[23] we would not say he was skipping.

IV. COMPARISON OF HOPPING AND SKIPPING

We can now state the significant similarities and differences between hopping and skipping. Both are combinations of mental action (an intention) and ongoing activity. Each has to do with locomotion.

---

19. I shall say nothing about twisting.

20. I am reminded that one of my best friends is called "Scooter". He prefers "Charles".

21. This does not detract from the fact that some are.

22. I rejection the suggestion that "Skipper" derives from either "skipping waves" or a sailboat's "skipping along".

23. See footnote 12, *mutatis mutandis.*

But whereas hopping involves either vertical motion or a combination of vertical and horizontal motion, skipping always involves a combination of vertical and horizontal motion. Hence, vertical and horizontal motion are necessary, but not sufficient conditions for skipping; this is because vertical and horizontal motion are permissible, although not necessary (nor sufficient) conditions for hopping. The same follows for the use of two legs (forgetting horses, not to mention the feats of millipedes). It is a necessary condition of skipping that it be done with two legs, but it is not a sufficient condition, for one can also hop with (on) two legs (although doing so is neither a necessary nor a sufficient condition for hopping). The relevant distinction seems to lie in the fact that skipping requires the alternative motion of first one leg, then the other. Hopping, however, requires the use of one leg only, and if both are used, they move together.[24]

V. CONCLUSION

I have now come to the end of my task, having distinguished between what we mean when we say "I am hopping" and what we mean when we say "I am skipping". It has been shown that hopping and skipping are intimately related as forms of intentional

---

24. It might be said now that while this distinction may distinguish hopping from skipping, it does not distinguish skipping from walking. This is perfectly true. But, it is not true, as has been facetiously suggested, that it does not even distinguish hopping from skipping. That is, walking is not just "hopping from one foot to another with an overall forward motion of the body". This is more like an *incorrect* description of running, than of walking. but I cannot carry these matters further now; in my book-length examination of ordinary walking I shall consider all normal forms of (land-bound) human locomotion—running, crawling, jumping, leaping, squirming, hopping, skipping, and groveling—in discursions on the present model.

action and overt activity, and indeed, the fact that hopping is a part of skipping has led us to the significant discovery of a potentially misleading metaphorical usage of "Skip it" when we mean literally "Hop it".

3

What *Does* It All Mean?
(The 1970s)

What *does* it all mean? More precisely, what is the source of the meanings conveyed to us by—or that we find in—various things in the world? I argue that meanings depend on what interpreters bring to a semiotic situation; that meanings are taken rather than given; and thus that meanings are subjective, relative, looser than we often think, and ephemeral.

Let us begin with the intentional fallacy.[1] This is the fallacy of assuming that the artist's intent is most relevant, or even relevant at all, in the interpretation of a work of art. Whatever the poet intended, for example, the poem in hand must be evaluated and interpreted—unless you want to commit the fallacy—only for what it is in itself. Whatever value or significance it has must show itself in the work itself. One can, of course, check to see if an artist did manage to convey what he intended to, but the work is not better or worse—is not to be evaluated—according to the success or failure of this intent. This suggests that meaning or significance can pertain in something independently of its producer's intent. So why not consider whether or not there is *anything* whose meaning *is* dependent on intent?

It would seem that the intent of legislators is necessary as carried out through federal acts for a specially printed piece of paper to have the value of one hundred dollars. One might claim that this piece of paper enters into public commerce and plays its role only through the intent of the legislators, and that this intent is crucial in the interpretation of the piece of paper as a one hundred dollar bill. It might be thought to be absurd here to attempt to evaluate or interpret this piece of paper without taking its authors' intent into consideration. For the interpretation of a work of art, the artist's intention may be at best suggestive, in fact irrelevant, and at worst misleading. But what would the one hundred dollar bill be without the legislators' intent?

There is a deeper question: What is the piece of paper even *with* the legislators' intent? For what is required is not only that they intend it to *be* a one hundred dollar bill, but that people *take it to be one*. And this can fail to happen, as has happened with the Susan B. Anthony dollar. Legislators intended this coin to be a medium of exchange in ordinary commerce, but people in general refused to take it as such. Now suppose that inflation got so bad that in a consumers' revolt, people started treating one hundred dollar bills as one dollar bills without federal intent in a *de facto* devaluation of the dollar. Something like that has already happened as people discard pennies and do business to the nearest nickel. What if inflation got even worse? People might start using gold nuggets as the medium of exchange, in opposition to federal intent.

For something to be what a one hundred dollar bill is supposed to be, then, the intent of legislators is not required. This is not exactly like the irrelevance of the artist's intention to the interpretation of a work of art, but it does show that the artifactor's intention need not be crucial in the evaluation or interpretation of the significance of an artifact.

Now let us go to an underlying concern here. Works of art and one hundred dollar bills are artifacts, produced on purpose by human beings. They have significance. But gold nuggets which are not artifacts also can have significance. Gold nuggets are not so much given significance when used unofficially as a medium of exchange, as they are taken to have significance. So gold nuggets can have significance with no one intending them to have significance. Does this mean that we have established that art objects and other artifacts can have significance independently of any intent that they have significance? Can something in general have significance independently of anyone's intending it to be significant? Apparently so.

Now for the deepest question. If something has significance independently of intent, then is this significance intrinsic in it?

Apparently the New Critics think that there is intrinsic significance in a work of art.[2] But surely no one would claim that gold nuggets are intrinsically units of exchange. What is special about works of art is that they were made on purpose. Is this what makes them significant? To claim this would be to commit the intentionalist fallacy again. The view that art objects have intrinsic significance conflicts with the method of the New Critics, but the view that art objects are not intrinsically significant greatly undermines the authority of the New Critics.

We have reached an important question about the underlying nature of things. Can a thing be something that it is not intrinsically? That is, can it have a nonintrinsic characteristic? Obviously it can. Being seen is not intrinsic to a tree but a tree can be seen, and when seen has the characteristic of being seen. So a gold nugget that is not intrinsically a medium of exchange can have the characteristic of being a medium of exchange. Does it not follow that a work of art could have significance without having that significance intrinsically?

What else can things be that they are not intrinsically? Something can be a good example. It can be a good example of things of its type. Is it intrinsically a good example? No. Intrinsically it is just similar in various ways to other items of its type. Furthermore, it can become a good example without anyone's intent to set it up as a good example, but simply because someone takes it to be a good example, the way a tree has the characteristic of being seen because someone is looking at it. Notice lots of things are seen without anyone intending to see them. This goes both for natural things and artifactual things, and especially for things that were not made to be a good example. Intent on the part of anyone is irrelevant to its being a good example or not. As a good example, it is just similar in various ways to other items of the same type. It is not intrinsically an example, good or bad. It can have the characteristic of being a good example merely on the grounds of being taken to be a good example.

How does this apply to significance generally? Significance is often given to things, but it is obviously adequate for a thing's having significance that it merely be taken to have significance.

Suppose someone sets up a pole with a crossbar on it as one end of a clothesline. After a while the lines are taken down, but the pole is left standing. Years go by and then a group of Christian pilgrims come by and see the pole with the crossbar. Some of them cross themselves, and others kneel before it to pray. Is this pole a religious symbol?

Next, the monkey at the typewriter. I prefer Pierre's cat, who often hits keys on purpose to annoy Pierre. Suppose one day in a *tour de force* Pierre's cat bats out a few strokes on the typewriter. Remembering the monkey story, Pierre glances at the paper in the typewriter and, to his amazement, recognizes the solution to one of the outstanding problems in logic, a solution heretofore unknown. Lucky Pierre?

Here is another. Suppose a vine grows in the pattern of 'DANGER' in front of a deep open pit hidden by vegetation.

Pierre, walking through the woods, sees the vine, and thinks, "Danger!" He leaps aside just in time to avoid falling into the pit. Is this not a marvelous mistake? Pierre mistakenly takes the vine to be a warning of danger because it resembles a word used to warn of danger, and the mistake is to his advantage. But what if the deep pit had been to the side where he leaped?

In neither the typewriter nor the vine case is there any intent that the result be significant. Nor is either situation like another old favorite: we see smoke and say, "Smoke means fire." No one intended smoke to mean fire. In itself, smoke means nothing at all. Smoke often does have a natural connection with fire, fire often causes smoke, and knowing this we say that smoke means fire. We take smoke to be a natural sign of fire, but this is usually only a way of saying that smoke is often caused by fire. In fact, there are no natural signs, for effects no more intrinsically signify their causes than do artifacts intrinsically signify the intent of their makers. Smoke is evidence of a cause, and an artifact is evidence there was a maker. But something does not signify its cause or maker unless we take it to.

Is the typescript case more difficult than that of the vine? It is as unusual for a vine to be used to convey meanings as it is unusual for typescript *not* to be used to convey meanings. (But maybe not in France, where vines are trained to grow and typescript is used as design. Once in Paris I saw a window full of brown clothes covered with this design: BULLSHIT.) In Pierre's cases, however, he takes as significant what is not intended to signify anything, and it is fair to say in each case that he is right.

No author or intent to signify is necessary for there to be signification. So where does the meaning come from? In each case, the observer invests what he sees with meaning. In the cases of the vine and the typescript, what no one meant to have signification, but which has the pattern of what is conventionally used to convey meaning or sense, is taken to have meaning (and thus is given meaning) by the observer. If intent that a thing have meaning is required for a thing to have meaning, we would have to say that the observer is mistaken. And we do talk of the vine case as involving a fortuitous (or disastrous) mistake, but the mistake is not one of mistaking the meaning. A vine, even one growing in the pattern of 'DANGER', has no meaning. The mistake is taking it to have meaning.

You might think the vine case is the more difficult. But in fact the typescript case is more difficult. In the vine case, nothing conceptually new is added. The observer knows the meaning of danger because he knows that people often do mean for 'DANGER' to mean "Danger!". But something conceptually new is introduced in the case of the typescript, the solution no one has ever conceived of before. Where did it come from? Not from the cat. How could the observer introduce it when he did not know it beforehand? Is it intrinsically in the typescript? One might, in fact, ask the same question about every new bit of knowledge or information one gets from typescript (or spoken words) in patterns one has never seen (or heard) before.

The answer to this has to be no, it is not intrisically in the typescript. It—this new meaning—has to come from the observer. The way it is usually thought to come from the observer is that the typescript that signifies this new solution is like a piece of a jig-saw puzzle made from a larger body of typescript that the observer has in mind and that conveys the context of the problem and a gap representing its solution. The cat's typescript—and the solution the logician reads off because he takes the typescript to be conveying something in a language he understands—fits into the gap in the context he brings to it. The observer contributes his understanding of the solution to the problem, once he sees something that can convey the solution.

But then does this typescript intrinsically convey that meaning? Or is it intrinsically characterized in such a way that it can *can* convey that meaning?

Here is an answer like that of philosophers such as Richard

Rudner.[3] Semiosis can take place in a diadic situation. That is, semiosis need not be triadic. For significance or meaning or value to be read or derived in a situation, there need not be three items: an endower of significance, an item endowed with significance, and an interpreter of significance—that is, a sender, a medium, and a receiver; there need be only a medium and a receiver, or, more precisely, an interpreter. No one need give meaning to anything, there need be no author, and no intention is required for a thing to be taken to have meaning or significance by and for an observer or interpreter. I have given several examples above of diadic semiosis.

But how is this possible? Obviously, like the logician and the typescript, these observers bring rules, keys, calculi, languages, patterns, templates, grammars, geographies, categorial schemes, theories, understandings, mores, customs, conditionings, cultural heritages, contexts, meanings, or just plain stories to the situation. If an observed item appears to fit into one of the stories they have in mind, they are very apt to take this item as being significant in the story. One of the stories we all know, for example, is that fire causes smoke. Another story we know is that something in the shape of 'DANGER' is often used to indicate danger. And some of us know logical calculi well enough to take a bit of typescript to signify a solution to a problem.

I should remark further on the typescript case. Wittgenstein of the *Tractatus* believed that certain patterns do intrinsically convey significance by showing logical form.[4] It is not that these signs tell us about logical space and logical form; they can't even be used by anybody to tell us about their form; these signs (Wittgenstein thought) have intrinsic characteristics that exhibit logical structures and make it possible for us to read off logical signification. They show form. But the program of developing an Ideal Language with which to show and tell clearly all that can be known has more or less been abandoned because Gödel proved that such a language cannot be complete.[5] There is, however, another reason for suspending the program. The forms, or the geography, of logical space are not palpable, and so if they are to be signified they have to be signified through a medium, usually marks on paper or vocal noises. And although the early Wittgenstein apparently thought that some patterns of marks or noises intrinsically signify these logical forms by having arrangements that exactly express or show them (Locke would say that the forms of the sentences exactly resemble—and Aquinas would say they are identical with— the logical forms), Wittgenstein also depended on a notion of variables according to which any mark or noise can stand for anything (Aristotle and Aquinas would say that they depend on a notion of unformed or unsignated matter that in itself can be or signate anything because in itself it is or signifies nothing).

To make a long story short, anybody who thinks that to be is to be the value of a variable[6] is still seduced by the view that something in marks and noises intrinsically conveys some truth that necessarily applies to existents. But on the whole, Western philosophers have pretty much abandoned the view that the representation of something either does or must resemble or display or show or picture what it represents; they have abandoned the view that anything intrinsic in marks or noises or their patterns or arrangements is necessary to the conveyance of significance by those marks or noises. Given that some marks and noises are known to be significant (although one has no clue as to what they signify), Western philosophers have abandoned the view that one can read off the significance of these marks or noises by examining their intrinsic characteristics. In other words, anything can be used to represent or signify anything, and if all you know is that something is a sign, you cannot from it alone discern anything at all about what it signifies. The hard thing to take here is that this goes for *Principia Mathematica* as well as for mysterious signs and portents in the desert sky. A logician who sees the solution to a problem in a fortuitously observed set of marks sees it only because he brings to it the structure of an entire language. In themselves, those marks signify nothing. Was this not once decided about names? Is this not an old story?

Where did we get the language? In the same way.[7]

If the author or any intentional attribution of meaning or significance is basically irrelevant, or at least unnecessary, to something's having significance or meaning, how important is the observer who takes something to have significance? Can something have significance if no one takes it to have significance? Presumably things intended to have significance are taken to have significance by their authors. But what if the author of a poem is dead and the poem is in a book unknown to anyone now living? Does it have significance? And what if a one hundred dollar bill flies off the printing machine and falls into a crack where no one ever sees it? And what if no one ever comes across the abandoned clothesline pole, or no one ever sees the cat's typescript? Each of these items has potential significance in the contexts of general stories or systems of understanding into which these items could be incorporated if observed by people who knew the stories. Of course this does not amount to much, for in this sense everything has potential significance, which is just another way of saying that anything can represent anything. A ideal example of this is the phenomenon of paranoia.

Let me take the story further. Suppose the human species becomes extinct and these items remain. Do they now have significance? We can bring in archeologists from outer space who find the poem, the one hundred dollar bill, the typescript, and the clothesline pole. These aliens are not human, but they are self-conscious, rational, language-using beings. They crack the code, learn the language, reconstruct Western culture, interpret the poem, understand the solution to the logic problem, recognize the one hundred dollar bill, and take the clothesline pole to be a religious symbol.

All right, then, let us eliminate all self-conscious, rational, language-using beings from the universe. What then? Are the poem, the typescript, the bill, and the pole still significant? Yes. The crux is that they are part of *my* story. Hylas thought nothing was "more easy than to conceive a tree or house existing by itself, independent of, and unperceived by, any mind whatsoever." But Philonous pointed out that it is a "contradiction to talk of *conceiving* a thing which is *unconceived.*"[8] Philosophers have tried to get out of this by calling it a predicament (which it is) and by using quotation marks, but no one can escape the story. Even if one could escape it, then if these items do not intrinsically signify anything, and if there is no one to take them as significant, surely then they are not significant.

At this point the first big gong tolls for the meaning death of the universe itself. The meaningfulness of the universe is pretty precarious if it depends on mortal beings like ourselves taking it to mean something.

Berkeley, of course, would not accept this result. He said that what we now call sense data are the words of God and that their display is God speaking to us. Our task is to learn this language of God, that is, we are to be natural scientists and learn how the world is put together.[9] This Berkeleyan view is in full opposition to the position I take here, for not only is the intent of the God-Author essential to signification for Berkeley, His words and sentences consist of the things themselves that are thereby intrinsically significant (although God could have given them significances different from those they now have). Berkeley's God-ordained world is certainly comfortable. It is a world that is only one way, *the* way.[10]

But what if there is no God? The course of my discussion, that is, the course of contemporary philosophy, is propelled by the view that there is no God. Or if there is a God, He is irrelevant. Even supposing God created the universe for a purpose, if every thing in the universe can represent anything, and no thing in the universe intrinsically signifies anything (and it is Descartes,[11] prior to Berkeley, who takes intrinsic significance out of the world by granting that God can give the world any signficance He wants, or none), then we are not going to be able to read off God's message. Even if we decide that the universe is an effect of a cause and that the cause is God, all we know is that there is a cause. Knowing the cause of something is not to know its significance. The cause of something is not its significance. We don't know why He did it. *Why did He do it?* We are still in the dark.[12]

Of course philosophers and theologians other than Berkeley have taken the universe as God's text. The trouble here again is that the significance of this text depends on the story or framework brought to it, and radically different significances have been proposed in the contexts of different stories. The universe as text requires—as does the Bible—a key for interpreting its significance, and there are many keys. What would you wager that your story is the key one?

Continental philosophers seem most adept at this kind of reading. Heidegger takes language itself to have intrinsic meaning.[13] Lévi-Strauss exposes the transformational structures underlying cultural behavior.[14] Foucault discovers the underlying epistemes of cultural institutions.[15] And Derrida sees anything at all as a text to be read.[16]

Lévi-Strauss can be criticized because others interpreting the same materials with his methods find different structures. Foucault can be criticized because it is easy to underpin cultural institutions with epistemes entirely different from the ones he proposes. And Derrida can be criticized for being an outright fictionizer. All of these criticisms are based on a presumption that these Frenchmen are willing to submit themselves to the scientific test of public objectivity. They're not. They don't care. Lévi-Strauss does grouchily claim scientific status, but complains that nobody else is capable of comprehending and applying his method. Foucault admits that other epistemes will organize his data, but insists on his superior choices. Derrida says let a thousand alternative readings of texts bloom (although he is a bit queasy about some readings of Heidegger).

Goodman speaks of the ways of the world.[17] Like Heidegger, Lévi-Strauss, Foucault, Derrida, and others, Goodman opens a prospect on infinite perspectives. Could he, the New Critics, and deconstructionists be belittling the intent of God and other artists just to impose their own intent on the world and art works? Are critics more important than artists? Did they rub out God and other authors to elevate interpretation? It makes sense. The same skeptical objections that destroy claims to knowledge of God's intentions apply to claims of knowledge of human intentions. The problem about discerning the artist's intention has been reduced to the general problem of discerning anybody's intention. But we can still take things to have significance. That's what critics do. For interpretation.

In any event, it does seem to be established that the semiotic relation is diadic. Anything can have signification, can be taken as significant in a context of understanding that is brought to it by an observer or interpreter. No one else need have intended that a thing be significant, and a thing need not be an artifact to be significant. Even if there were an author or artifactor or a God, there is no certain way of figuring out that intender's intent. The interpreter's intentions are the only relevant ones. The interpreter becomes the artist or author or God.

But where does what we bring to the world come from? Kant[18] and Chomsky[19] say that we are born with the schemata or the deep grammar with which we understand the world and find things significant. They, like Descartes, Locke, and Hume, assume that all members of the human species share essentially the same categorial or conceptual or referential or grammatical framework; that we all bring more or less the same story to the world; and thus that all of us will take things to have significances at least similar enough to one another that we can get along. In fact, the wars of dogma, religion, and ideology show that there is a considerable looseness in the template.

Probably human understanding involves such a template fitted to the world, but obviously it can accommodate many different and even conflicting stories. I conclude that meanings are subjective and relative because various interpreters take things to have different meanings in the contexts of the different or even the same[20] frameworks they use to comprehend the world. Meanings are ephemeral because—so far as we know—all interpreters are mortal. We are the source of the meanings of the various things in the world. It all means what we take it to mean.

NOTES

1. W. K. Wimsatt, Jr. and Monroe C. Beardsley, "The Intentional Fallacy," *Sewanee Review* 54 (1964): 468–488; reprinted in W. K. Wimsatt, Jr., *The Verbal Icon* (Lexington: University of Kentucky Press, 1954), pp. 3–18.

2. Gerald Graff, *Literature Against Itself* (Chicago: University of Chicago Press, 1979).

3. Richard S. Rudner, "Show or Tell: Incoherence Among Symbol Systems," *Erkenntnis* 12 (1978): 129–151.

4. Ludwig Wittgenstein, *Tractatus Logico-Philosophicus,* trans. by D. F. Pears and B. F. McGuinness (London: Routledge & Kegan Paul, 1961), #2.2, etc.

5. Ernst Nagel and James R. Newman, *Gödel's Proof* (New York: New York University Press, 1958).

6. Willard Van Orman Quine, "On What There Is," in *From a Logical Point of View* (Boston: Harvard University Press, 1961), pp. 1–19. See also the extensive literature stemming from this article first published in 1948.

7. Cf. Noam Chomsky, *Cartesian Linguistics* (New York: Harper & Row, 1966).

8. George Berkeley, *Three Dialogues Between Hylas and Philonous* (La Salle: Open Court, 1955), p. 48.

9. Ibid., p. 91.

10. *Pace* Nelson Goodman, *Ways of Worldmaking* (Indianapolis, Ind.: Hackett, 1978).

11. René Descartes, *Meditations on First Philosophy,* in John Cottingham, Robert Stoothoff, and Dugald Murdoch, *The Philosophical Writings of Descartes* (Cambridge: Cambridge University Press, 1984), Vol. 2, pp. 1–62.

12. See "The Seducer and the Seduced" in the present volume, pp. 69–88.

13. Martin Heidegger, *On the Way to Language,* trans. by Peter D. Hertz (New York: Harper & Row, 1971).

14. Claude Lévi-Strauss, *The Elementary Structures of Kinship,* trans. by James Harle Bell, John Richard von Sturmer, and Rodney Needham (London: Eyre & Spottiswoode, 1969); *The Raw and the Cooked,* trans. by John and Doreen Weightman (New York: Harper & Row, 1969); *From Honey to Ashes,* trans. by John and Doreen Weightman (New York: Harper & Row, 1973).

15. Michel Foucault, *The Order of Things* (New York: Pantheon, 1971); *The Archaeology of Knowledge,* trans. by A. M. Sheridan Smith (New York: Pantheon, 1972).

16. Jacques Derrida, *Of Grammatology,* trans. by Gayatri Chakravorty Spivak (Baltimore: Johns Hopkins University Press, 1976); *Writing and Difference,* trans. by Alan Bass (Chicago: University of Chicago Press, 1978).

17. Nelson Goodman, *The Structure of Appearance* (Indianapolis, Ind.: Bobbs-Merrill, 1966); *Ways of Worldmaking* (Indianapolis, Ind.: Hackett, 1978).

18. Immanuel Kant, *Critique of Pure Reason,* trans. by Norman Kemp Smith (London: Macmillan, 1933).

19. Noam Chomsky, *Cartesian Linguistics* (New York: Harper & Row, 1966), and in many other works.

20. Cf., for example, Willard Van Orman Quine, *Word and Object* (Cambridge, Mass.: MIT Press, 1960).

4

The Seducer and the Seduced
(The 1980s)

"A deception is a rather ugly thing."
—Søren Kierkegaard

ADAM AND EVE

Innocence sullied is a primal theme of Western culture. In the Story of Stories, the serpent seduces Eve, who in turn seduces Adam. Seduction leads to blame, for when the Lord God came walking in the garden and found that Adam and Eve knew they were naked, he asked if they had eaten of the forbidden fruit: "And the man said, The woman whom thou gavest to be with me, she gave me of the tree, and I did eat. . . . And the woman said, The serpent beguiled me, and I did eat" (Gen. 3:12–13). When I read this story to my seven-year-old daughter, she said, "But *God* made the serpent."

JOB AND ABRAHAM

Among the sons of God was Satan, who spent his time going to and fro in the earth, and walking up and down in it. The Lord bragged to Satan about Job, the most faithful of the faithful. And then Satan the son of God tempted God to permit him to tempt Job. God gave Satan leave to try to seduce Job. Satan thus seduced God but he failed to seduce Job. Job was had, but it was ultimately by God.

When I read the story of Job to my daughter—who incidentally thought it one of the greatest stories ever told—she was outraged from beginning to end. "God is not fair!" she would interrupt.

But she calmed down to ponder the end. Job was given more than he had in the beginning. And he was given seven sons and three daughters. "Were they the *same* that were killed in the beginning?" she asked.

"No," I said. "They were new ones."

My daughter gave me a look of unmitigated scorn, slid off my lap, and marched off not saying a word. The next day I bribed her to listen to the story of Abraham and Isaac. After she heard the story, she said indulgently, "God's not real, is he? They made him up, like Santa Claus."

The story of Job does not make sense. Neither does that of Abraham and Isaac. God promised Abraham that He would make a nation of the seed of Isaac, but then He said: "Take now thy son, thine only son Isaac, whom thou lovest, and get thee into the land of Moriah; and offer him there for a burnt offering upon one of the mountains which I will tell thee of" (Gen. 22:2).

Did it amuse God to tempt Abraham? Did it amuse Abraham to be tempted? Seduction can be a lot of fun for both the seducer and the seduced. Abraham is usually thought to have passed the test. But was he seduced nevertheless? Suppose that Abraham was a knight of infinite faith. And that so was Job. Suppose that they believed despite contradiction. *Credo quia absurdum.* And then?

The reasoning of a little child is like a steel trap. My daughter knew that Job and Abraham had been had. By God. Because what He did to them makes no sense.

Søren Kierkegaard yearned to be a knight of infinite faith. He strove to escape the viscous hold of the aesthetic and the ponderous rationality of the ethical. But he thought too much. *"Don't think!"* was God's command, and Kierkegaard admired Abraham for not thinking. But Kierkegaard himself could not stop thinking. What worried him was the thought that he was being made sport of, that he was being diddled, fucked over, by God.

Listen to Kierkegaard in *Fear and Trembling:*

I

When the child must be weaned, the mother blackens her breast; it would indeed be a shame that the breast should look delicious when the child must not have it. So the child believes that the breast has changed, but the mother is the same, her glance is as loving and tender as ever. Happy the person who had no need of more dreadful expedients for weaning the child!

II

When the child has grown big and must be weaned, the mother virginally hides her breast, so the child has no more a mother. Happy the child which did not in another way lose its mother!

III

When the child must be weaned, the mother too is not without sorrow at the thought that she and the child are separated more and more, that the child which first lay under her heart and later reposed upon her breast will be so near to her no more. So they mourn together for the brief period of mourning. Happy the person who has kept the child as near and needed not to sorrow any more!

IV

When the child must be weaned, the mother has stronger food in readiness, lest the child should perish. Happy the person who has stronger food in readiness![1]

In every version the child is fobbed off.

These tales are appended by Kierkegaard as quaint explananda accompanying four versions of the story of Abraham and Isaac. All are recitations of deception.

In the first, Abraham pretends to be an idolater in order to prove Isaac's faith in God, as the mother merely blackens her breast to retain her child's love. But this is to usurp God's prerogatives; it is to think one knows more than God; it is to fail the test. The deceiver deceives also himself.

In the second, Abraham does not tell Isaac that God has asked for the sacrifice, but instead takes the burden upon himself, losing Isaac's love as the mother who hides her breast loses her child's love. Again, they think they know more than God, concealing His ways, deceiving the child and themselves.

In the third, Abraham laments openly, allowing Isaac to see his distress, laying the blame on God. But the decision to comply

---

1. *Fear and Trembling,* trans. Walter Lowrie (Princeton: Princeton University Press, 1941), pp. 12–15. All subsequent quotations are from this edition.

is Abraham's, just as the mother who mourns with her child that they must part chooses to follow the ways of man. They deceive the child by not taking their share of the blame.

Finally, in the fourth, Abraham betrays his despair, causing Isaac to lose his faith, just as the mother substitutes the rankness of meat for the sweetness of milk to wean her child. The stronger food is atheism.

Kierkegaard's stories about Abraham and Isaac are inconclusive. None of them makes clear what God wants. Christ does not know either. On the cross, he says, "My God, my God, why hast thou forsaken me?" (Matt. 27:46). God sent his only *begotten* son to earth and left him in doubt. Again—as with Job and Abraham—the story continues. Christ is resurrected to sit on the right hand of God. But does that make sense? Christ was considerably less firm than Abraham and Job. Christ was not even a knight of infinite faith. At the end, Christ did not even trust God. Kierkegaard didn't either. Trust implies expectation of a reasonable degree of consistency.

JOHANNES AND CORDELIA

Here is the course of a notorious seduction as outlined in Kierkegaard's "Diary of the Seducer," the crowning glory of *Either/Or*. Johannes attracts Cordelia's attention by convincing her that he has been captivated by her charms. He becomes engaged to her, but then teaches her to despise public bans and bonds. The mediation of society and the church prevents the direct expression of true love. Cordelia gains strength and seeks autonomy. She breaks the engagement and conceives the plan of seducing Johannes. Cordelia becomes the active instigator of her own seduction. In the end, Johannes need only lie back and let it happen.

But did Johannes do it to Cordelia? Deflower her, I mean.

Why not set her up and let her down?

Johannes runs away from Cordelia on the night of her capitulation—just as Kierkegaard ran away from Regine, for whom he wrote "Diary of the Seducer." Johannes writes:

> Why cannot such a night be longer? If Electryon could forget himself, why cannot the sun be equally sympathetic? Still, it is over now, and I hope never to see her again. When a girl has given away everything, then she is weak, then she has lost everything. For a man guilt is a negative moment; for a woman it is the value of her being. Now all resistance is impossible, and only as long as that is present is it beautiful to love; when it is ended there is only weakness and habit.[2]

Here is the key passage: "Now all resistance is impossible." Does this mean she surrendered her virginity? Surrender, yes, but Johannes need not take the prize. It is enough that she no longer resists looting.

It would be out of character for Johannes to copulate with Cordelia. Throughout the "Diary" he builds a fairy-tale world for her. In his entry the day before the fateful night, he says, "Everything is symbol; I myself am a myth about myself, for is it not as a myth that I hasten to this meeting?" She was seduced, but only figuratively screwed.

---

2. *Either/Or,* trans. David F. Swenson, Lillian Marvin Swenson, and Walter Lowrie, 2 vols. (Princeton: Princeton University Press, 1944), I, 439. All subsequent quotations are from this edition.

DON JUAN AND JUDGE WILLIAM

If Don Juan had sexual intercourse with 1,003 Spanish women without, as one of my students exquisitely put it, getting calloused, it is because Don Juan lives in the present. A brainless butterfly, flitting from flower to flower, Don Juan is always in the ecstasy of orgasm. He has no memory of the past, of other women; he is always enveloped in the loving cup of anywoman, reduced to atemporal phallic thoughtlessness by erotic intoxication. With no memory of the past and no thought of the future, Don Juan is not even a person. He is nothing more and nothing less than a state of perpetual sexual satisfaction.

The alternative is presented by Kierkegaard through Judge William, who argues that it is a man's duty to marry. The married man is a personality. He lives in time, remembers the past, and plans for the future. He is a grown-up. If Don Juan is the pure essence of the aesthetic, the married man is the paradigm of the ethical. Spontaneous and spectacular sensual delight gives way to the calmly measured comforts of conjugal love.

What an utter bore, thinks the young man "A" to whom the Judge's nostrums are addressed.

Repetition is a bore. And what a bore always to be deflowering virgins, come to think of it (as Don Juan does not). Don Juan does not know what a Lothario he appears to be, and if it were not for Leporello keeping count, there would be no one to brag for him. Don Juan has no memory. But what good is it to be in sexual bliss if you can't even remember from moment to moment? This is why women forgive Don Juan. He's just a big baby. He's not even self-conscious.

The ultimate boring situation is Christian marriage. The emblem of boredom is the faithful spouse. How does an honest young man avoid the Scylla of prosaic marriage without being drawn into the Charybdis of mundane promiscuity?

He could masturbate. Take up "Diary of the Seducer." Notice

the rhythm. It is particularly strong in the letters. Johannes keeps building up tension, and then holding back. "Diary of the Seducer" is one of the greatest masturbation fantasies in Western literature. There is only one way to prolong the pleasure. Don't come. If Johannes went all the way with Cordelia, and then with another Cordelia, and another, he would get bored. If he married Cordelia, he would get bored. Either/or.

Kierkegaard says that if you do the one, you'll be sorry, and if you do the other, you'll be sorry. In the continuous orgasm, Don Juan is drained of sensibility. In Judge William's family orgasm, sexual excitement is denatured. Kierkegaard urges us to transcend the aesthetic of Don Juan and the ethical of Judge William. Rise to a state of secret ecstasy, but don't go over the top.

SØREN AND REGINE

On 10 September 1840, Søren Kierkegaard was formally engaged to Regine Olsen. On 11 October 1841, he broke the engagement. Four days later, he fled to Berlin, where he began a four-year stint of incredible creativity. *Either/Or* (including both "Diary of the Seducer" and Judge William's long letters to the young man "A") was produced during this period, as well as *Fear and Trembling, Repetition, An Essay in Experimental Psychology,* and several other works.

Let us not mince words. Kierkegaard's central problem is the adversary relationship between God and man. He concludes that God demands a direct, exclusive union of man with God. Marriage interferes for two reasons. It diverts love, devotion, and duty away from God and directs man toward woman. And because marriage is a sacred union in which no secrets can be kept, it elevates a woman to a role that rightfully belongs only to God. When is one justified in breaking an engagement? Only when he has a secret so awful that it can be revealed only to God. Kierkegaard had such a secret. He broke the engagement with Regine.

Never think that Kierkegaard was not really attracted to women. Listen to this:

> My eyes can never weary of surveying this peripheral manifold, these scattered emanations of feminine beauty. Each particular has its little share, and yet is complete in itself, happy, glad, beautiful. Every woman has her share: the merry smile, the roguish glance, the wistful eye, the pensive head, the exuberant spirits, the quiet sadness, the deep foreboding, the brooding melancholy, the earthy homesickness, the unbaptized movements, the beckoning brows, the questioning lips, the mysterious forehead, the ensnaring curls, the concealing lashes, the heavenly pride, the light step, the airy grace, the languishing posture, the dreamy yearning, the inexplicable sighs, the willowy form, the soft outlines, the luxuriant bosom, the swelling hips, the tiny foot, the dainty hand.—Each woman has her own traits, and the one does not merely repeat the other. And when I have gazed and gazed again, considered and again considered this multitudinous variety, when I have smiled, sighed, flattered, threatened, desired, tempted, laughed, wept, hoped, feared, won, lost—then I shut up my fan, and gather the fragments into a unity, the parts into a whole. Then my soul is glad, my heart beats, my passion is aflame. This one woman, the only woman in all the world, she must belong to me, she must be mine. Let God keep His heaven, if only I can keep her. (*Either/ Or,* I, 423–424)

I grant that this passage is buried four deep. There is Kierkegaard who wrote it, then the editor Victor Eremita, then the young man "A," and finally Johannes himself, the purported author of "Diary of the Seducer" and of these words. Still. . . . The passage rivals anything in Shakespeare as a panegyric on the desirableness of woman, and surpasses Goethe in its awful defiance of God. It is the hair that does it—those ensnaring curls that loop about a man, make him eschew heaven, and drag him down to hell. Hair like a snake.

Satan is peanuts compared with woman as God's rival.

Suppose you follow my interpretation, but then give me the horse laugh, saying, "Bah! He just couldn't cut the mustard, that's all."

Don't be deceived. Kierkegaard was no namby-pamby, no Peter Pan, no secret admirer of little girls or boys. Mustard-cutting is Kierkegaard's own vernacular. Perform the reversals, execute the transformations. You can't make Kierkegaard wince. Look at this:

> Conjugal love . . . seems so mild and heartfelt and tender, but as soon as the door is closed behind the married pair, then before you can say Jack Robinson out comes the rod called duty. (*Either/Or,* II, 147)

A man who can make a terrible joke like that is crude, *gross.* But Judge William's claim that marriage is a duty is just as outrageous. On the other hand, maybe *it* is a duty. He has just defined conjugal love as "faithful, constant, humble, patient, long-suffering, indulgent, sincere, contented, vigilant, willing, joyful." But *boring.* It's "an everyday occurrence." Let this *man* Kierkegaard quaff his *aqua vitae,* puff his cigar, lean over, dip his pen in the inkwell, and write down a story for Judge William to tell:

> "How disgusting it is," you say [Judge William is putting words into the mouth of the young man "A"], "to see the languor with which such things are performed in married life, how perfunctorily, how sluggishly it is done,

almost at the stroke of the clock—pretty much as among
the tribe the Jesuits discovered in Paraguay, which was
so sluggish that the Jesuits found it necessary to ring a
bell at midnight as a welcome notice to all husbands,
to remind them thereby of their marital duties. So everything is done on time, as they are trained to do it." (*Either/
Or*, II, 143)

A vulgar joke? But forty years in anticipation of Pavlov—how
about that? And don't laugh at a terrified man.

Why is the joke funny? Is it that a real man needs no reminder?
Jack Robinson is always ready for action? Hah, hah—belling sex,
indeed.

It's a terrible joke. The Jesuits never rang bells to remind men
of conjugal duties; they rang them to remind men to attend church.
Man's only duty is to God. The horror of it is that a man *is*
like Pavlov's dog, conditioned to salivate at a woman's smell.

In *The Unbearable Lightness of Being*, Milan Kundera presents
some speculations of his Don Juan figure, Tomas: "He thought:
In the clockwork of the head, two cogwheels turn opposite each
other. On the one, images; on the other, the body's reactions.
The cog carrying the image of a naked woman meshes with the
corresponding erection-command cog."[3] It is, of course, a double
entendre. On the one hand, the sight or thought of a naked woman
makes old Jack Robinson pop up whether it is socially convenient
or not, and on the other hand, nothing (no bell, no smell) ever
makes it certain that one can rise to the occasion. Kundera again:

In the fourth century, Saint Jerome completely rejected
the notion that Adam and Eve had sexual intercourse

---

3. *The Unbearable Lightness of Being*, trans. Michael Henry Heim (New
York: Harper & Row, 1984), p. 236. All subsequent quotations are from this
edition.

in Paradise. On the other hand, Johannes Scotus Erigena, the great ninth-century theologian, accepted the idea. He believed, moreover, that Adam's virile member could be made to rise like an arm or a leg, when and as its owner wished. We must not dismiss this fancy as the recurrent dream of a man obsessed with the threat of impotence. Erigena's idea has a different meaning. If it were possible to raise the penis by means of a simple command, then sexual excitement would have no place in the world. The penis would rise not because we are excited but because we order it to do so. What the great theologian found incompatible with Paradise was not sexual intercourse and the attendant pleasure; what he found incompatible with Paradise was excitement. Bear in mind: There was pleasure in Paradise, but no excitement. (p. 246)

Enough beating around the bush. As the actress said to the bishop, "Enough making love; off with the pants." Masturbation is a sin, sexual intercourse outside marriage (and in marriage for recreation) is a sin, and wet dreams are the result of sinful dirty thoughts. Alas, even presidents commit adultery in their minds (and some in the White House). The point is this: God made man with a thorn in his flesh. God gave man an agonizing desire for woman. And then God says: "That's a no no. Nasty, nasty, mustn't touch."

GOD AND MAN

Paul the Apostle says:

It is good for man not to touch a woman. Nevertheless, to avoid fornication, let every man have his own wife, and let every woman have her own husband. . . . But

I speak this by permission, and not by commandment.
For I would that all men were even as myself. . . . I say
therefore to the unmarried and widows, it is good for
them if they abide even as I. But if they cannot contain,
let them marry: for it is better to marry than to burn.
(I Cor. 7:1–2, 6–9)

Earlier, there are conflicting stories in Genesis. The good-guy story
goes as follows: "God created man in his own image, in the image
of God created he him; male and female created he them. And
God blessed them, and God said unto them, Be fruitful, and
multiply" (Gen. 1:27–28). Presumably, then, Adam and Eve are
to reproduce. But in the bad-guy story, procreation comes explicitly
into the picture—and with a vengeance—only after the snake is
reeled out. Before disobedience, Adam and Eve "were both naked,
the man and his wife, and were not ashamed," but after disobedience, "they knew that they were naked" (Gen. 3:7). Then
God gets huffy:

Unto the woman he said, I will greatly multiply thy sorrow
and thy conception; in sorrow thou shalt bring forth
children; and thy desire shall be to thy husband, and he
shall rule over thee. And unto Adam he said, Because
thou hast harkened unto the voice of thy wife, and hast
eaten of the tree, of which I commanded thee, saying,
Thou shalt not eat of it: cursed is the ground for thy
sake; in sorrow shalt thou eat of it all the days of thy
life. (Gen. 3:16–17)

As Judge William says, "the marriage service proclaims that sin
entered into the world along with marriage" (*Either/Or,* II, 92).
Only with knowledge of sex did sin arise.

POPEYE AND OLIVE OYL

Popeye's prick is enormous and erect. Olive Oyl lies on her back, knees up, cunt gaping. In his haste, Popeye trips over his prick and falls burying his face—pipe and all—in Olive Oyl's cunt. "Ooooo, Popeye!" Olive Oyl coos.

Jiggs fucks Maggie, too. These comic books were drawn over fifty years ago, but are still selling even in these days of glorious color photographs of split beavers and standing tools. Can you believe it? Men still get off on Mickey and Minnie Mouse. Classics never go out of print.

Kierkegaard's upright young man is repelled: "Love as such [i.e., the lunacy of sexual desire] . . . appears to me as ridiculous, and hence I fear it, lest I become ridiculous to myself or ridiculous in the eyes of the gods who fashioned men thus."[4] All men fear the appearance of being ridiculous. Nothing is more ridiculous than a man trying to convince a woman to let him have his way. In "The Banquet," Kierkegaard has the young man give a speech on the absurdity of love. Here is the absurdity: the inexplicability of a man's attraction to any woman is universally accepted as a satisfactory explanation of the phenomenon. Preposterous behavior is countenanced in an otherwise rational man by reference to the notorious blindness of love.

Olive Oyl, Maggie, and Minnie are not even good-looking. The drawings themselves are crude, as though done by a sweating adolescent while playing pocket pool with his left hand. Dirty little boys, OK. But the *embarrassing* thing is that this trash has the power to arouse grown men.

Sexual desire is uncontrollable. Never mind Olive Oyl. Kierkegaard's young man says: "If it is ridiculous to kiss an ugly girl,

---

4. *Stages on Life's Way,* trans. Walter Lowrie (Princeton: Princeton University Press, 1940), p. 51. All subsequent quotations are from this edition.

it is also ridiculous to kiss a pretty one." Engaging in sexual congress might be all right if one chose to do it, he continues,

> but to be a marionette in the service of some inexplicable power is comic. The contradiction is that no one sees any rational reason why it should get a twitch now in one leg, now in the other. When I cannot explain to myself what I am doing, I don't want to do it; when I cannot understand the power to whose sway I am about to commit myself, I don't want to commit myself to its sway. (*Stages,* p. 54)

An incredible, ludicrous confusion results. What takes place, the young man argues, is an

> erotic reversal whereby the loftiest experience in one sphere [the spiritual] does not find its expression in this sphere but in another sphere [the carnal] that is the polar opposite of the first. It is comic that the high flight of love (the desire to belong to one another for all eternity) constantly ends like Saft [a glutton] in the pantry; but still more comic is that this conclusion of the affair is supposed to be its highest expression. (*Stages,* p. 55)

The purpose of a pornographic comic book is perfectly plain. It is a crutch used to overcome a man's limp so he can come to climax. There is no confusion here: the occasion is completely carnal. In fact, all a man really need to look at to compensate for the lack of a compliant woman is a triangle with a line splitting it. Little boys draw them on the walls of rock shelters while they tend the sheep in Galilee today; men drew them on the walls deep in caves 40,000 years ago.

Kierkegaard's young man is sure that women don't really understand. The reason is that they are entirely carnal. What they offer has nothing spiritual about it. Consequently, the young man says, "Only gods and men [know that love combines contradictory elements], and hence woman is a temptation which is meant to entice men to be ridiculous" (*Stages,* p. 59).

That wouldn't matter, except for Kierkegaard's conviction that as the opposite of the spiritual which leads to salvation, the carnal is the open pit of hell. The lure of sex is so strong, moreover, that man has confused woman with the true object of spiritual love. Our duty is to love God, not a woman. The very monstrousness of the juxtaposition of the seat of "love" and the site of urination ought to be enough to warn a man that something is fishy. The itch of sexual desire and the tickle of its satisfaction are the antithesis of spiritual exaltation. How could *anyone* be so stupid as not to see through this vulgar outrage against faith and reason?

Popeye and Jiggs are as helplessly tumescent as dogs blindly pursuing a bitch in heat, and are just as likely to be run over by a passing Juggernaut. They respond like puppets to every female sign. This is what is funny—and terrifying—about their plight.

The pornographic pages turn in the silence of intense concentration. It is eerie, this suction that pulls a man, blind and deaf, down the vortex of sensual oblivion. What is a man's *most* private moment? When is he most furious at interruption? When he is ministering to his private parts.

JESUS AND MARY

Priests and nuns don't do it. What they lose in public esteem by lack of experience they gain in awe of their abstinence. Their power and authority are bolstered by their resistance to sexual temptation. Anyway, priests learn plenty from confessions.

It is undignified to exhibit interest in prurient subjects. Not to put too fine a point on it, it is undignified to have a hard-on. To bring down the great man, catch him *in flagrante delicto.* Dignity is so anti-sexual that it handicaps the seducer. Here, a snatch of flirtatious conversation:

> She: "Oh, Mister Johnson, I just can't help it! I keep thinking of you as 'Mister Johnson.' " (*Substitute:* Sir, Professor, Doctor, Reverend, Father, Colonel, Lord, Boss, etc.)
>
> He, unbuckling his belt: "Well, heh, heh, we know how to cure you of *that,* don't we?"

And it *does* cure her. Exposure to his unruly little penis, his red-faced puffing as he huffs the house down . . .

> When Adam delved
> And Eve span
> Who then
> Was the gentleman?

Never mind that Celia's shitting quashed Swift's lust: Mary fucked would scuttle salvation. Jesus, the son of the virgin, is sexless. And dignified. *And saved!*

Christ did not marry. Christ did not sin. If we were all to imitate Christ, then there soon would be nobody. God told Adam and Eve to multiply, but fucking is a sin. I ask you . . .

Kierkegaard was tormented with the thought that indulging in desire for woman was to enter the maw of hell. Here is a prohibition with teeth in it. It was not God's intent that man should know himself naked. Yet God did pipe up the serpent in the garden and bring to consciousness a need so strong that man gives up heaven to satisfy it. Lust runs rampant in mankind. Concupiscence is a really dirty trick.

It's entrapment, that's what it is. If a man's bells weren't set to ring every time a woman pulled his rope, it would never have occurred to him to play her tune. But his sexual triggers are so delicate that the wind from every flapping skirt pulls them off. He is outraged at his inability to put salacious thoughts aside when a man should be concentrated on important matters. He doesn't *want* to be aroused by every woman who passes by. He doesn't *want* to blush and sweat and get a hard-on. He *despises* himself when he jerks off.

At the reckoning he can shout: "It's not fair! Thou makest a man hungry, ply him with meat, then condemn him because he doth eat."

Pathetic.

Kierkegaard was very sensitive about venereal matters. There is the story that in his cups he once was taken by friends to a whorehouse where he did the manly thing. I don't believe a word of it. Toward the end of his life, when he *knew* he would die soon, he became euphoric. He was convinced that he had finally become a knight of infinite faith. I think this was because he had been chaste, and now was sure he was going to hold out to the end. He was finally too sick to fuck and fall.

THE SEDUCER AND THE SEDUCED

Why do so many men fall for the despicable myth that women secretly enjoy being raped? I wonder if it is not because there is a desire in all of us to be seduced. If one is seduced, then one is not really responsible for the fall from grace. "He tricked me. . . . He promised. . . . He made me do it. . . . I am not to blame."

We are often justly suspicious of these excuses (not in rape, but in seduction). What business had the victim putting her virtue in jeopardy? Cordelia set out to seduce Johannes, but failed. And if later she pleads—"He didn't do it! I'm still a maid!"—who would not smirk? Johannes knew. He had only to get her into position. That was enough. Set up, traduced, and abandoned. What matter the actual act? Her lack of resistance did for it all.

Johannes never touched her maidenhead. As the young man "A" says of him:

> He had known how to tempt a young girl and attract her to himself, without really caring to possess her . . . he knew how to excite a girl to the highest pitch, so that he was certain that she was ready to sacrifice everything. When the affair reached this point, he broke it off. (*Either/Or,* I, 303)

And Johannes himself says near the end of the "Diary":

> Simply and directly, to betray a young girl, that I certainly could not endure; but that the idea is set in motion, that it is in its service that I act, to its service that I dedicate myself, that gives me self-discipline, abstemiousness from every forbidden enjoyment. (*Either/Or,* I, 432)

Johannes the idealist flees from Lorelei's earthy song. Cordelia's virginity is preserved. And Johannes?

GOD AND KIERKEGAARD

It's a contradiction. God giveth and taketh away in one unmoving motion. It makes no sense. Satan and the snake, the instruments of seduction, are God's creations. God is the original con man. He sets us up for the sting. Kierkegaard waited for the payoff all his life.

Kierkegaard worried. Would God take him or not? He was ready, like Cordelia, to be had. He'd *been* seduced. Now he wanted *it*. But maybe God rode off without consummating the match. Kierkegaard was always spreading, but God never seemed to want to nail him. Kierkegaard despaired in fear of ultimate rejection. You roll over, and the seducer leaps back and laughs. And runs away?

In the end? There is still the final engagement, not the little death, but The Big One. Kierkegaard approached it trembling like a spinster to her wedding bed. Let's hope he got what he wanted. A deception is a rather ugly thing.

5

How to Die
(The Pits)

Before you read this personal essay, you doubtless want to know what my philosophy is. And in two sentences. Very well, let me say that I find these to be peculiar times. Some of us live the most extraordinarily satisfying lives in a century that has witnessed the genocidal slaughter of six million Jews; a world in which atom bombs have been dropped on Japanese cities, in which torture is common, and in which hundreds of millions of people live in conditions of abject poverty, starvation, oppression, and hopelessness. The leaders of the Soviet Union and the United States seem determined to go to war with one another sooner or later, and they have enough nerve gas and germs (never mind the panoply of nuclear, hydrogen, and neutron bombs) to wipe us all out. My daughter, who is twenty, thinks someone will push the button, and she asks me what we can do about it. I don't know. Probably nothing. My wife, who is an archeologist, says there have always been winners and losers. Some of the earliest written records are about atrocities of war. For example, the key text for cracking the cuneiform code is a description of what Darius did to rebels in the fourth century B.C. He cut off their ears, put out their eyes, cut off their noses, and then dragged them behind his chariots in chains.

But you wanted to know my philosophy. It has to do with form and content. This philosophy is derived primarily from my Welsh mother and my Scots father. When I was very young, my mother used to sit beside me to make me practice the piano. "Let's get on with it," she would say. My father also had a saying. When I sought sympathy after stubbing my toe or falling down and skinning my knee, he would say, "Rub dirt in it." Two sentences.

So let's get on with it.

*   *   *

In the dark of the cave, we had come to the pit we had to cross. The three of us crouched in an opening the size of a picture window, peering twenty feet across to the passage that continued on the other side. The light from our carbide lamps did not reach the bottom, but we tossed in rocks to guess that the pit was maybe fifty feet deep. No one had been down it. No one had been very far along the passage across it. We were exploring.

Bill was having trouble with his carbide lamp, so he sat down behind us in the passage to work on it. Dave started across the pit on a narrow ledge while I watched. Halfway across the pit Dave's body overbalanced. He fell slowly away from the wall, turned completely over in the light of my lamp, and disappeared into silent blackness. He didn't say a word. Eons later there was a quiet thud.

I had been told by the first explorers that there was a crack in the floor of the passage on the other side that might lead to the bottom of the pit, but I was across the pit and had chimneyed twenty-five feet down the crack before I knew what I was doing.

All the while I was yelling to Dave that everything would be all right. I didn't believe a word of it. I knew that my old friend was dead.

The last ten feet to the bottom of the pit seemed to be sheer, smooth limestone wall. As I reached it I heard Dave groan. Unbelieving, I just let go and slid the rest of the way down.

He lay on a thirty-degree slope of mud with his head pointing down. He had fallen flush on the slope between two large pointed boulders and had slid down until his head was at the edge of a deep pool of water. He was bleeding from a cut where his hard hat had smashed against his ear, but there seemed to be no broken bones. "I'm all right," he said, and stood up. We climbed back up with the help of Bill reaching down, and the three of us crossed the pit at the top again. That was enough exploring for one day. Four hours later we were outside.

On another trip into the cave, we measured Dave's fall: forty-four feet.

After that fall, Dave and I continued to explore caves for many years. Or I should say that we continued to explore a cave, for we were in the Flint Ridge Cave System in Kentucky, then the second-longest known cave in the world. We were trying to climb the Everest of world speleology. Our quest was to connect the Flint Ridge Cave System with Mammoth Cave, the third-longest in the world. (The longest was Hölloch in Switzerland.) If we made the connection, the resulting system would become the longest cave in the world. We worked on it weekends, holidays, and summers for twenty years before the connection was made. Roger Brucker and I wrote a book about it: *The Longest Cave*. At the time the connection was made, the only active explorers who had stayed with it for the entire time were Roger and I. Neither of us was a member of the final party that made the connection.

There were other incidents like Dave's fall, but of the several hundred serious cavers who explored and mapped the 144 miles of cave passages in that cave system during those twenty years, not one was badly injured or killed. I have often wondered why not. Caving is basically underground mountaineering on muddy rocks in the dark, and in Flint Ridge you are taking the chance of being killed. You accept the odds.

Why?

Because exploring the great cave—learning the skills that few others possess and going places where no other human being has been and where few others will follow—is something that fills your soul with everlasting joy and with memories that nothing but total senility or death can ever efface.

All it required was total commitment for a few years, or perhaps, if you slipped once too often, for a lifetime.

I don't suppose many of you want to explore a big cave or climb a high mountain or sail around the world. These are adventures to read about, though. There ought to be something *you* can do that is as satisfying and doesn't require highly specialized skills or putting your life in danger.

I'm talking about form.

The crucial thing is commitment. And the content does matter. It could be mountain climbing, or jogging, or dieting. They're all hard to do. Jogging is popular because it's so simple. You can run anywhere. Unlike football, baseball, tennis, or even skiing, the difference between what you are doing and what the world-class runners do is not all that great. To improve your status, all you have to do is move down the road a little faster.

I want to compare here the commitment involved in someone who decides to climb Everest with the commitment required to stay on a diet, say, to lose twenty pounds and keep them off. The words seem almost tangible as I search for just the right ones so this transition does not appear to be grotesque, ludicrous, and absurd.

Reinhold Messner and Peter Habler were the first two human beings to climb Everest without oxygen. Messner thereafter continued to push himself to the limits of his, indeed to the limits of human, capacity. A few years later he became the first human ever to climb Everest without oxygen, *alone.*

Absolutely incredible.

And Messner is still pushing.

"He'll cash in one of these days," a friend said to me.

"Of course," I replied. "He knows it."

Is it right to commit yourself to an activity in which you know the end result will be death? Of course it is. It is, after all, right to commit yourself to life.

If you would like to do one difficult thing in your life that requires total commitment, something that if accomplished would fill you with joy and satisfaction for the rest of your life, then the content matters; but it is the form that carries you through, the form that counts.

As for content, there are two rules: whatever you do, try to have fun doing it. And try not to hurt anyone.

Losing twenty pounds and keeping them off for the rest of your life is as good a content as many. Don't knock it. Don't let other people knock it. Dieting doesn't put you out there on the edge of the pit where one false step means oblivion, but in some ways it is harder than exploring big caves and climbing high mountains. The weight game is not one that lasts for only a few years, after which you can retire gracefully with your laurels and get fat. It lasts a lifetime . . . and there are no laurels.

But what about Messner and those like him who push it until they peel off a wall? This essay is, after all, about how to die. My answer, as you can guess, is that you should endeavor if at all possible to die with class. People pushing limits, like Messner, have at least the satisfaction of knowing that if they die in the act, it will be in good form.

Suicide? Don't be absurd. They don't want to die. They don't intend to die. They choose to do something very difficult right at the limits of human possibility in order to savor the joy and satisfaction of having done it. The risk is essential. It defines how hard it is. Even more, the risk of death raises awareness of life to a peak. Socrates said, Know thyself. On the edge we are reminded of our mortality, knowledge of which makes us human.

I'm afraid that the fun of exciting, risky games also leads us to war. There are individual skills involved in fighting, but when you take as your adversary another human being rather than a mountain or a cave, you have hit upon an instance when content changes the form of the game. Mine is a game of self-control and self-reliance. In war you abandon yourself to those who order you to kill. I ask you to be fanatical about leading your own life. In war, fanatics allow themselves to follow a leader— and everyone gets hurt.

While writing this essay, I have thought many times of the philosopher Richard Rudner. He was the chairman of my department and I think he hired me in part because it amused him to call me Doc Watson.

On sabbatical in the south of France, Rudner became aware of a severe pain in his back. Local doctors could not diagnose it, and since Washington University has as good a medical school as any in the world, Rudner flew home to St. Louis to have a checkup. He was told that he had cancer throughout his body, and that if it was not arrested, he had about three months to live.

They gave him chemotherapy, which inhibits the growth and division of cancer cells. Unfortunately, it does the same for white blood corpuscles that fight infection. Rudner lasted six weeks before he caught a blood infection and died. He was fifty-seven.

This led to the following exchange. A good friend was lamenting how Rudner had died in full middle age.

"Middle age?" the wag he was talking to said. "Jerome, no one lives to be a hundred and fourteen."

Rudner would have loved that wisecrack. It was made by one of his old students. Only a couple of years later that student himself died of cancer at the age of forty-seven. Both he and Rudner would have appreciated the irony.

Rudner died in elegant form. He was working on a book and was corresponding with other philosophers. In great pain and nausea, he continued to put his papers together, to wrap things up in preparation for the inevitable. He fought like hell to continue the life he enjoyed so much. He remained the village atheist to the end and expected nothing beyond.

A few hours before he died, he told his family he would see them tomorrow. He didn't.

I know that one of Richard Rudner's greatest regrets before he died was that he had not completed the book he had been working on for many years. Of course, he was anguished at not being able to grow old with the woman he loved, at not being able to see his grandchildren. But I think he would sigh tolerantly and approve of the point I'm going to make with his story; and he would have said with that pained look on his face he got whenever I piled pomposity on platitude, "You tell 'em, Doc." It is this:

Write your book before you die.

To write is to die a little. It is a good way to go. It is like having children. You created them, but once they go their own way, there is nothing much you can do about it. Sometimes it is nice to think that they will still be yammering on, after you yourself are gone.

Write your book before you die. You will get great satisfaction from it.

That's the form of the thing. The content is any serious expression of self that does not harm others. It takes some dedication, some commitment. It is taking control of part of your life to shape it as you will.

For those philosophers who think that mind and body are identical, that matter is all that exists, my program ought to be a piece of cake. Its content, however, may not appeal to them. Some of the best philosophers were fat. Plato means Fatso.

Let me tell you how David Hume died. In his youth he was a lean, hawkish fellow who began to eat himself silly after undergoing an extreme skeptical crisis during which he despaired of ever finding truth. He never found truth, but he was a fat, jolly fellow the rest of his life, and a champion player of whist (an early form of bridge). He once said that in ordinary life one should exercise clever prudence and common sense. Philosophy should be done only in the closet. There is no question in my mind that when he said this he winked broadly to his card companions and made an exaggerated gesture with his chins in the direction of the W.C.

The French bluestocking ladies loved Hume and called him *le bon David: le grand bon vivant, David Hume.* What he died of was probably stomach cancer, which gripped his gut and wasted him away. He took it in good grace, encouraged his friends to visit him in his sickroom, and told them to cheer up.

The reports of Hume's good spirits and demeanor much disturbed another of the great characters of the eighteenth century, James Boswell, the famous biographer of Dr. Johnson. Boswell was disturbed because Hume was a notorious atheist, and it was not right that an atheist should go cheerfully to his doom. Boswell himself was a Christian, and a believer, who greatly feared for the salvation of his own soul because of his weakness for lying and whoring. He could not rest until he saw Hume.

Who knows how Hume felt physically on the day of Boswell's descent? It surely did not matter. *Le bon David* knew why Boswell was there, and he rose to the occasion. Never had he been so gay, so witty, so droll. He parried Boswell's every probe; and with every cheerful quip, he sank Boswell's hopes for heaven farther toward the depths of hell. Boswell went home in such a state of depression that he himself took to bed. And lo, he had a dream. He dreamed that Hume had recanted and confessed, and had died in the arms of Jesus. It wasn't true, of course, but Boswell could not bear thinking of the alternative.

David Hume died in excellent form.

After a funeral you have a big meal. Food and fat are not

just symbols of life, they sustain it. To deny them is to deny a little bit of life. If you take off twenty pounds and keep them off, you will often be reminded of the way it must be in the end.

I'm not sure how you are going to weather this heavy writing. I treat hellfire and brimstone elsewhere in this volume. This is the part in which you find out for whom the bell tolls.

What I have to say is that fat, my friends, is in my book a metaphor. Fat represents the nagging triviality, the utter banality, and the inevitability of ordinary reality that separate us from what we think we want to be. It is the fleshly part of ourselves that binds us to this earth and keeps us from eternal life. My thesis is that the myth of heavenly paradise is but a dream of attenuated earthly joys abstracted from the trials and tribulations of daily life.

Render out some of that fat. Get down to the muscle. Bare yourself to the rising wind. I have said before and I will say again that it really does not matter much to the rest of us what you do, so long as you don't hurt anyone. But if you don't do something you will be proud of later on, it will matter to *you*.

Take hold and fight.

You can do it even if your father was not Scot, nor your mother Welsh.

My father starved to death in his eighty-first year of life. "Mark 1980," he said. "It's a bad year." It was for him.

The Omaha surgeons disagreed about what went wrong in his gut. There was a tumor, but evidently not a malignant one. After the tumor was removed adhesions closed his bowels. Another operation. Then adhesions blocked the kidneys. Another operation. They finally got a straight shot through his gut, but he had had it. "Let's get out of this place and go home," he said.

Instead of going home, we moved him to a small community hospital a few miles from the school in which he had taught most of his life. Everyone there knew him. One of the nurses was the daughter and granddaughter of two women who had graduated from the New Market High School when my father was superintendent. He still needed a lot of care and he knew it. At least he was close to home.

When my father was settled in his bed, he said to the doctor, "I don't want any more of those goddamned tubes down my nose or needles in my arm." They glared at each other. They had known each other for over forty years, two dominating and authoritative men in that small, rural Iowa community, used to being looked up to, used to being obeyed.

The doctor looked down and said, "You know what that means, Prof."

My father said nothing, but nodded with grim satisfaction. The doctor turned to me. I shrugged my shoulders. He walked out.

I spent the last three weeks of his life with my father. When I arrived, he called me over and said, "Now Dick, I'm dying. Don't give me any crap that I'm not.'"

"OK," I said, "so you're dying. Now what?"

He just closed his eyes and grinned.

His mind was, as they say about those who die from eating the Destroying Angel mushroom, clear to the last.

A few days before he died, a favorite niece and her husband visited him. As they got up to go, the husband said, "Now Prof, I want you to be sitting up in a chair next time I see you."

My father reared up in bed with the old diabolical leer in his eyes and said, "You don't see too many people buried sitting up, Giles."

I tried to feed him and he tried to eat. He could get a little down, and it went on through. But it wasn't enough.

He gagged. He hated the mashed chicken. "Chicken feathers," he would say when I would sneak in a bite. "I don't want any more of those damned chicken feathers." He would drink a bit of chocolate milk.

One late afternoon, in the last slanting light of a sunny winter's day, my father asked me to help him turn over on his side. I did and said, "Is that better?"

"Hell no, it isn't better," he said. "You always did ask the dumbest questions."

I sat back down with my book.

In a little while he said, "It's all right."

About fifteen minutes later I noticed that he had quit breathing.

*   *   *

Here are some things my father loved to eat. Bread and milk. The bread was fresh out of the oven, grainy and moist, the hard shiny crust scented with lard that had been smeared on it for glazing. The milk was fresh and warm from his old Jersey cow. My father liked a thick slice of bread, and he did not break it up. He folded it once and shoved it whole into the glass of milk, then smashed it down and ate it with a spoon. When I was a child I would watch him, and sometimes he drooled on purpose and rolled his eyes. "Watson, stop that!" my mother would say.

My father liked to take a big chunk of butter churned from the cream of his old Jersey cow, put it on a bare plate, pour sorghum molasses on it, and smash the mess up into a foam with a fork. Then he would spread the whole onto a thick slice of bread. The molasses crusted, the butter cut its sweetness, and the taste was like ambrosia.

My father liked Missouri Wonder beans—not your common Kentucky Wonder bean, he would say, but the Missouri Wonder that he had brought with him when he moved north to Iowa in 1922. He liked a fresh pan of beans to be half green pods and half shelled, boiled with a lot of small chunks of bacon. He would eat this with shining white slices from a raw winter onion as large as an apple. Hot beans, salty bacon, and cold, sweet onion. Never did a man eat so good.

My father grew tomatoes, which he sliced and ate raw with salt. He bottled thick tomato juice for winter. He liked to put several spoons of sugar into a glass of tomato juice, drink the juice down an inch or two, then fill the glass to the top again by adding milk. Stir. Drink.

My father raised four kinds of grapes; three kinds of apples; peaches and plums. He raised strawberries, black and red raspberries, blackberries, boysenberries, gooseberries, and currants. Rhubarb, turnips, kohlrabi, sweetcorn, popcorn.

My mother made jelly from the black raspberries, and my father liked to spread thick, yellow butter and great globs of black-raspberry jelly on his bread. The gooseberries were for gooseberry pie. The rhubarb was boiled thick and eaten with much sugar and cream. He liked to eat turnips and kohlrabi peeled and raw. He slathered butter on sweetcorn and poured so much melted butter on popcorn that your fingers grew slippery while eating it.

My father was a great hunter and fisherman all his life. He like catfish dipped in cornmeal batter and fried in deep lard. He liked squirrel gravy.

My mother made noodles and cooked them with pot roast. She fried chicken. She baked bread. She fed my father.

My father liked . . . he liked to eat. I don't know what he liked best of all. Probably bread and milk. That was what he asked for most during the final days of his life. But maybe what he liked best was gravy made from ham grease and mixed with cream. He would take a thick slice of bread, put it on his plate, and spoon on ham gravy until all the bread was soaked through. The thin gravy ran all over the plate. My father would eat the soaked bread quickly, then mop up the rest of the gravy with more bread. I can see him now, hunched over his plate, jerking his chin up sharply to catch some gravy running down and threatening to drip on his shirt. He grins at the small boy across the table and takes another bite.

"Oh, Watson, stop that!" my mother says, and my father's joy is complete.

6

Ape Dreams
(The 1990s)

The first adult book I remember having noticed as a child was *Tarzan of the Apes*. It was on a shelf jammed with books in the dark hall at the top of the stairs. It was also the first adult book I ever read, when, as best I can estimate, I was about seven years old. There were a dozen other books by Edgar Rice Burroughs on that shelf—fifty years later I still have them—and I read them all. They were my father's books, although I never saw him reading them. To escape his life as superintendent of schools in a rural Iowa town of 350 people, he read shoot-'em-up westerns.

I also remember seeing the movie *Tarzan Finds a Son*. The boy was running from something—a lion, I think. Sticking up from the ground in a burned-over area were stubs of small trees like pointed wooden stakes two feet high. If he tripped and fell, he would be impaled. Then there was this giant spider web, strands thick as ropes, and the boy got trapped in it. Enormous, hairy, black spiders bore down on him, and . . .

All right, I confess. I saw *all* the Tarzan movies, and I remember one thing clearly: There was always a chimpanzee. That came back to me the other night when I saw a new play titled *Ape and Apple* by Stephen Dierkes. It was about a young woman who had been abandoned in the jungle by her father—she had been trying to get him to stop drinking and had poured out all his whiskey. She would have died if an ape man had not fed her fruit. They had a son who grew up to be a perfectly normal young man. One day he brought home the woman he wanted to marry, and darned if she wasn't a chimpanzee.

In the Tarzan movies the chimpanzee was always great. It clowned a lot, and warned when lions were about. But was it boy or a girl? Why was it called Cheeta? Cheater? I never noticed whether or not Tarzan was attracted to female apes—I mean, there was Jane—but then all through my youth I also missed what was going on between Hopalong Cassidy and Lucky. I always thought it sad that neither of them ever got the woman. The reruns are really embarrassing.

But what about chimpanzees?

In 1953, the Book-of-the-Month Club chose as one of its selections a novel titled *You Shall Know them* (Boston: Little, Brown) by the French writer Vercors. Its dust jacket reads in part as follows:

> *What is man?*
>
> At the bar of justice, his life hanging on the answer, stands Douglas Templemore, journalist and thinker, lover of mankind, and father—for science's sake—of several infants, *possibly* human. . . .
>
> Not far off, Derry, the strange creature who mothered the "son" that Douglas killed, is quartered happily in London Zoo. Not science nor philosophy, nor Parliament

nor clergy, can decide if she is manlike ape or apelike man.

Yet the court must rule. For if man can be defined, and if Derry fits the definition, Douglas has committed murder. But if Derry is judged ape, her whole race is condemned to legal slavery—precisely what Douglas is trying to prevent.

Vercors imagined the discovery of a tribe of primates that constituted the missing link between apes and man. They had low IQs but could talk. To save them, Vercors' hero showed— delicately, by artificial insemination—that they could interbreed with human beings, and thus were persons like you and me.

That's pretty heavy stuff, and well before the animal-rights movement. On the other hand, those strange creatures are a lot like chimpanzees. Of course if they *had* been chimpanzees, the novel would never have made the Book-of-the-Month Club.

In 1963, Pierre Boulle published *Planet of the Apes* (New York: Vanguard), which became one of the most popular science-fiction novels and movies of all time. I remember a wonderful scene in the movie in which the female lead chimpanzee (Kim Hunter) permits the male human hero (Charlton Heston) to kiss her cheek. She giggles and shudders because he is so barefaced ugly. We all know it was Kim Hunter, right? Still, she made one cute chimpanzee. So we're getting close.

Here it is, the keystone passage from Bernard Malamud's apocalyptic last novel, *God's Grace:*

With a waxed twine inserted through the eye he had punched into a nail, he sewed together the two halves of the dress; and Cohn considered adding a pair of white drawers, but gave that up when it occurred to him they would only get in the way. When Mary Madelyn, groggy from outrunning pursuing males all day, returned to the cave, Cohn presented the white garment to her as a friendship gift.

She asked what she could do with it, and Cohn said he would like her to dress in it, and he would help if she needed help. Apparently she didn't. She went through the motions of clothing herself and seemed to enjoy dressing, though she had never before in her life worn any garment except a hat of flowers she had once made for herself.

Cohn, stepping back to admire her elegant appearance in the white dress, said she looked like somebody's bride.

"Do I wook wike Juwiet?"

"Sort of, though I'm no Romeo."

"I wov you, do you wov me?"

"Sure enough," said Cohn. "I sure do."

Perhaps her eyes misted, perhaps not, but it seemed to Cohn that she would have cried a little if chimps could. Maybe someday—another step in their humanization.

Turning the lamp low, he proposed that she and he mate, and Mary Madelyn modestly assented.

He lifted her white skirt from the rear, and with shut eyes telling himself to keep his thoughts level, Cohn dipped his phallus into her hot flower. There was an instant electric connection and Cohn parted with his seed as she possessed it. He felt himself happily drawn clean of sperm. Mary Madelyn was at once calmed. She waited a minute for more to happen, but when nothing more did, she chewed up a fig and fell asleep on his bed.[1]

Mary Madelyn, the chimpanzee who could talk because of surgical intervention on her vocal cords, did conceive a child with

1. Bernard Malamud, *God's Grace* (New York: Farrar, Straus & Giroux, 1982), pp. 168–169.

Cohn, the last man on earth. It was the best he could do to save humanity, and it isn't as though we weren't prepared for it.

King Kong abducted a maiden with lust in his eye, but the most disturbing sex scene in recent ape movies occurs in *Greystoke,* a 1984 film subtitled *The Legend of Tarzan, Lord of the Apes.*[2] In Malamud's novel, to bring the chimpanzee up to a human cultural level so he can have intercourse with her, Cohn dresses her. He would have undressed a woman. In *Greystoke,* Tarzan works himself up to mate with Jane, and as he rages and rackets about the house finally to race up the stairs and burst into her bedroom, he is entirely chimpanzee. How they mate is not shown, but the symbolism in *Greystoke* is obvious. Tarzan comes out of the jungle for a while, but, perhaps like the human species, he surfaces into civilization only for a moment, and then sinks back into bestiality at the end of the movie. When he returns to the jungle, there is no real indication that he will ever come back (although, of course, there are always sequels to Tarzan books and movies). And what about Jane? You know the languid, stretching-in-bed morning-after scenes in movies. She liked it.

So far, the most poignant novel of love between man and chimpanzee is John Collier's *His Monkey Wife, Or, Married to a Chimp.* The chimpanzee, Emily, is treated throughout as a very delicate and fastidious maiden. The language of the last scene in the novel conveys the tone of the entire enterprise:

> When at last the evening's merriment was done, and Mr.
> Fatigay and his bride had been escorted to the dear house
> in which they had first met, which had been swept and
> garnished to receive them, they sat a long while on the

---

2. All of the actors who played chimpanzees in this film (along with the actor who played Tarzan) were trained to hunker around like apes by Roger Fouts, who for many years has been teaching Washoe and other chimpanzees to use American Sign Language.

verandah, watching the lights in the village fade out one by one, and the moon rise like a clear and simple idea in a happily tired mind. Not a word was spoken. They almost ceased to think.

"Well, we must to bed," said Mr. Fatigay at last, and rising reluctantly, he switched on the light. Home, with chairs and tables, sprang up about them, like a comfortable wooden cage for the nocturnal feelings, shy as birds, which the blue moon-silences had lured from out their timid hearts.

Soon afterwards, Mr. Fatigay came from his room and sat on Emily's little white couch, wherein she sat upright, dark and dainty as a Spanish princess.

"Emily!" he said, and was silent for a long time.

"Emily!" he said. "My Angel! My own! My love!"

At this last word, Emily raised her eyes, and extended to him her hand.

Under her long and scanty hair, he caught glimpses of plum-blue skin. Into the depths of those all-dark lustrous eyes, his spirit slid with no sound of splash. She uttered a few low words, rapidly, in her native tongue. The candle, guttering beside the bed, was strangled in the grasp of a prehensile foot, and darkness received, like a ripple in velvet, the final happy sigh.[3]

Why is the hero named Fatigay, a transliteration of the French word for fatigued? He does pursue a woman who evades him for years, and he finally realizes that his chimpanzee servant is more loving and faithful than his fiancée. So maybe the novel is just an elaborate put-down by an author foiled in love. But I know nothing of John Collier's personal life. Maybe he married a lower-

---

3. John Collier, *His Monkey Wife, Or, Married to a Chimp* (1931; reprint edition, Garden City, N.J.: Doubleday, 1957), pp. 258–259.

class woman, and this is his paean to her. On the other hand, maybe the novel is a thinly veiled defense of misogyny. But wait a minute, it was written in 1931. Could the chimpanzee have been a Jew? In any case, you can't convince me that it's just entertainment.

What is this fixation on chimpanzees all about? The answer is fairly obvious. When chimpanzees, gorillas, and orangutans were introduced to Europe during the eighteenth century, everyone thought they were just peculiar people. Linnaeus classified them as a kind of human being, and a female chimpanzee named Madame Chimpanzee was the toast of London in the winter season of 1738–39. She wore a dress, was said to be modest about exposing her sex, and was very polite at tea. But were these likable creatures really human beings?

In a footnote to his 1755 *Discourse on the Origin and the Foundations of Inequality Among Men,* Jean-Jacques Rousseau suggests the obvious experiment for finding out whether or not apes are men. He even points out that the production of a half-breed would not be enough to settle the matter. The offspring themselves would have to be mated to see if the cross breeds true. Only if it does can we be sure that apes are human.

A very similar question was asked and answered numerous times in human history when peoples of different morphological characteristics came together for the first time. Interbreeding between different species of human beings goes way back. The Neanderthals are now extinct, but in the present population of Homo sapiens there are people with Neanderthal features that could have gotten there in only one way.

I am under the impression—as are other scholars I have talked to—that during the eighteenth century experiments were actually made to see if apes could mate with Negro women, and that they failed, probably because the "apes" used were not true apes like us but baboons. But all I can locate in the literature are travelers' tales about apes lusting after women and abducting them. There is probably very little in most of these stories.

The base question is whether or not apes are people. Recently it has been claimed that apes are persons who merit some of the rights that human beings enjoy. A major argument for this is that because apes have demonstrated that they can communicate rather well using American Sign Language, they have one of the major defining characteristics of persons—they can use language. But this is disputed by some scientists and philosophers, and has not proved conclusive. What would prove that chimpanzees, say, are people? Well, we know. Suppose they were really just odd-shaped human beings, and. . . .

I know of only one contemporary report of a breeding experiment between apes and men. It may be a newspaper hoax, but it did give rise to discussion. In *Can Animals and Machines Be Persons? A Dialogue,* Justin Leiber presents the following hypothetical exchange:

MARY GODWIN: Biology is not a simple topic, particularly in this case. My geneticist friends tell me that, biologically speaking, humans and chimpanzees have in common more than 99 percent of their genes. Would you say, therefore, that because chimpanzees are 99 percent biologically human, they are 99 percent persons?

COMMISSIONER WAI CHIN: I do not think you want to rest too much on biological details. Such dependence has a disreputable history, for there are genetic variations among human "races" of a comparable sort, and I take it that you would not want to agree with those who have emphasized these variations. On strict biological grounds, humans and chimpanzees are more closely related than either is to gorillas; and all three species are closer biologically than any to the orangutan. Of course, some older secondary school texts give humans a separate biological family. But this is sheer nonsense biologically.

In the late 1960s, . . . I was expelled from my pro-
fessorship at Beijing University. The "cultural revolutionaries" of that time had me spend the next decade as a
farm laborer on the northeast, near Shenyang. I there
heard the curious story that some of my own country's
scientists had successfully impregnated a female chimpanzee with human sperm. They, too, were reeducated by
the cultural revolutionaries, so the experiment was stopped.
A decade later, when I became again respectable, I served
on a panel that set priorities in scientific research. I felt
no burning need to reinstitute the chimpanzee-human
experiment. It seemed to me a somewhat idle question.

Surely you don't say that everything depends on
whether humans and chimpanzees are close enough genetically to produce offspring? That if they can, then chimpanzees are persons, otherwise not? Could you mean this?[4]

Leiber references an actual newspaper article from the *Chicago
Tribune* reprinted in the *Houston Post* of 15 February 1981 (Section
A, p. 19) about the Chinese experiment, but he drops the discussion
about interbreeding. He dismisses the genetic argument that apes
are persons on the grounds that human beings have souls or selves
and other animals do not. But I think proof that interbreeding
is possible would be a powerful argument for the conclusion that
apes are persons—people like you and me.

Could humans and chimpanzees successfully interbreed?

No matter how curious you might be, wouldn't you feel dis-
tinctly uneasy in suggesting that the experiment be made? Maybe
it can be shown that interbreeding is possible without actually
producing any babies.

There are two key articles in *Science,* the American Associa-

---

4. Justin Leiber, *Can Animals and Machines Be Persons?* (Indianapolis,
Ind.: Hackett, 1985), pp. 6–7.

tion for the Advancement of Science weekly, that bear on the closeness of chimpanzees to human beings. "Evolution at Two Levels in Humans and Chimpanzees"[5] By Mary-Claire King and A. C. Wilson has as a subtitle: "Their macromolecules are so alike that regulatory mutations may account for their biological differences." King and Wilson point out that the genetic difference between chimpanzees and human beings is extraordinarily small, corresponding to the genetic difference between interbreedable sibling species of fruit flies and of mammals. Also, the genetic distance between some sibling species of frogs is much larger than that between human beings and chimpanzees. Sibling species are usually virtually identical morphologically, so why are human beings and chimpanzees so different? King and Wilson say that all biochemical methods show that the genetic difference is too small to account for the bodily difference, so they hypothesize that the differences are caused by different timing or levels of activity in regulatory mechanisms that influence embryonic development. So after finding that the genes are more than ninety-nine percent the same, they conclude that human beings and chimpanzees differ almost entirely in the way their bodies and organs develop. Such regulatory mechanisms in Scandinavians, for example, may differ slightly from those in Bushmen, and this would explain major bodily differences between them.

Jorg J. Yunis, Jeffry R. Sawyer, and Kelly Dunham also document the genetic similarities between chimpanzees and human beings in their article "The Striking Resemblance of High-Resolution G-Banded Chromosomes of Man and Chimpanzee."[6] The abstract of the paper reads: "The fine structure and genetic organization of the chromosomes of man and chimpanzee are so similar that it is difficult to account for the phenotypic [bodily] differences." They show that all chromosomes in humans and

---

5. *Science* 188 (1975): 107–116.
6. *Science* 208 (1980): 1145–1148.

chimpanzees are parallel. That human beings have 46 chromosomes and chimpanzees have 48 is explained by the fact that some chromosomes have fused in man that are separate in chimpanzees. This does not destroy their basic similarity.

There is much less genetic difference between chimpanzees and human beings than there is between horses and donkeys or between lions and tigers, species that interbreed successfully. The authors of the two *Science* articles conclude that, while the genetic difference between human beings and chimpanzees is greater than that between different human races, the genetic evidence very strongly indicates that human beings and chimpanzees can interbreed successfully.

This is a striking conclusion, still hypothetical, but based on very solid data. After finding this out, my first thought was: Why doesn't everyone know it? Although Commissioner Wai Chin in Leiber's fictional dialogue says that it seems to him to be a somewhat idle question as to whether or not human beings and chimpanzees can interbreed, it seems to me on the contrary to be a question with immense potential for challenging most religious, philosophical, and ideological pictures of the place of human beings in the cosmos.

Just to begin with, the successful interbreeding of human beings and chimpanzees could be the culmination of the Darwinian revolution in biology. It might have a greater impact on humanity than the Copernican revolution. It could have as much effect on the human psyche as the appearance of aliens from outer space. Thus, I look at the evidence that successful interbreeding is probable, and again ask: Why doesn't everyone know?

In his *Silent Partners: The Legacy of the Ape Language Experiments,* Eugene Linden suggests an answer to a very similar question. He asks why the great excitement and enthusiasm that greeted the first news that chimpanzees had learned sign language is now gone. Why do some psychologists today say that the idea that nonhuman apes use language is so preposterous that it does not even merit investigation? Or even if apes can use some language, they say it is of no scientific interest. Linden is surely correct in thinking that these attacks are based not solely on the scientific data, but are fueled in large part by religious and philosophical dogma. In his chapter entitled "The Unwelcome Mirror," he says that theological questions will have to be separated from scientific questions before we are going to get the truth about language use in apes.[7] (Linden also points out, by the way, that chimpanzees are in high demand now because they are the only common research animal that can be infected with AIDS.)

Apes are not the only animals that have to prove themselves. It is an anthropological truism that any isolated group of human beings will call themselves "people" and refuse this status to human beings who differ from them in any way. Thus it has taken some time for whites to agree that blacks are human beings, and for the Japanese to agree that the Chinese are human, and vice versa. The differences among human races barely show up, if at all, genetically, and we agree that all races are human. Now on the same ground of genetic similarity it can be concluded that human beings and chimpanzees (and probably the other great apes) are sibling species.

But does this show that humans and chimpanzees could inter-breed successfully? I don't know, but some biologists I've talked to say yes, of course. The most amazing thing is that they go on to ask, so what? Probably this is just the defense of professionals against sensationalism. Biologists should know as well as anyone that if the general public *also* knew, really *knew* that human beings and chimpanzees could successfully interbreed, all hell would break loose on the creationist front. If Darwinists and evolutionists want a knock-down argument, here it is.

Nobody is really going to believe it, of course, unless it is

---

7. Eugene Linden, *Silent Partners: The Legacy of the Ape Language Experiments* (New York: Times Books/Random House, 1986).

done. Should we do it? Merely by discussing it, am I in effect recommending it? Of course we could experiment with eggs and sperm in a test tube, just to see if it would take. Not conclusive, eh? What about Rousseau's second step? Real ape people would have to breed true.

So we have come to it again. Old Bern really had guts—he was a man with one tough psyche—to describe that scene of fornication between his hero Cohn and a chimpanzee. After all, the Bible forbids sexual congress between human beings and other animals.

But what about artificial insemination? Or suppose (ancient travel literature, fantasy fiction, comic books, and movies are full of such stories) a woman were raped and impregnated by a gorilla (a *most* unlikely occurrence, given that male gorillas are apparently not very highly sexed in the first place). How would that be handled by right-to-life advocates? Hey, don't ask me. I'm no theologian.

But as a strictly theoretical question, would it be wrong to produce such a cross? If it is biologically possible, then it is natural. And if it is natural, can it be wrong? It certainly could be, for there are many natural acts that human beings believe are wrong. Rape, for example. I suspect that a general view that it would be wrong to produce a human-chimpanzee cross—wouldn't it be a form of rape?—is a major reason why it has not been done. But from a naturalistic standpoint, would it be more wrong to cross human beings and chimpanzees than to cross horses and donkeys? We have already spliced human and pig genes to produce a very strange breed of pig for medical research—diabetes, that sort of thing. They are peculiar pigs. They just lie on their sides all the time, with haunted looks in their eyes. The pig breeders promise us that they won't let those funny pigs get into the ham market.[8]

---

8. Bill Lambrecht, "The Gene Revolution Promises New Problems: Gene Splicing Aims for Super Animals," *St. Louis Post-Dispatch,* 8 December 1986: 1A.

Surely it would be wrong to produce ape people if they were destined to be slaves or otherwise confined, in the same way that it would be wrong to breed tractable human beings with IQs of 70 to do the dirty work for the rest of us. It would be wrong in the way it is to produce castrati, who, one might suggest, given their lack of sexual hormones and sexual development, are more different in a crucial way from the rest of us than is a normal chimpanzee.

It is unlikely that apes and men would have been classified in different families if *we* had not been doing the classification. When alien scientists from outer space classify the animals of earth on the basis of genes, chromosomes, and DNA, they will lump human beings and chimpanzees as one species.

I have always liked chimpanzees. All the apes. You know, they are a lot like people. If everyone knew that in fact they *are* people, then perhaps we could save them from extinction. (But then, perhaps not.)

But should apes be given all the rights that human beings have? Why not? Apes couldn't do any worse with them than we do. In fact, apes in their natural state don't make war and commit general mayhem at anywhere near the same scale we do. Anyway, we should not rule out the possibility that if we improve our communication with the great apes, we might find them to be just as moral as we are.

Well, shall we do it? Oh, I don't know. But wouldn't it be, well, *interesting* to see what kind of creature the ape man would be? In nightmares and matinees we picture crosses between apes and human beings as malevolent monsters or moronic monstrosities. But maybe the child would overreach its parents. It might happen, you know.

POSTSCRIPT

Shortly before I received proofs for this essay, a report (again from the *Chicago Tribune*) appeared in the *St. Louis Post-Dispatch* (14 May 1987, p. 2) titled "Ape-man: New Subhuman Species Called Within Reach." Here are the key passages:

> Brunetto Chiarelli, dean of anthropology at Florence University . . . said this week that through refined techniques of artificial fertilization, biogenetic scientists are capable of making a new breed of slave, an anthropoid with a chimpanzee mother and a human father.
>
> Chiarelli said the experiments on the new subhuman species had been interrupted at the embryo stage because of "ethical problems". . . .
>
> In an interview, Chiarelli suggested that the new species could be used "for labor chores that are repetitive and disagreeable . . . or as a reservoir for transplant organs."
>
> He also said genetic researchers at Florence University had successfully crossed two species of ape—the gibbon and the siamang. "These two species are genetically more diverse than man and ape," Chiarelli added.

7

A Pig's Tail
(The End of the Second Millennium)

The text I am considering is a novel in English written by Gregory Rabassa[1] based on a novel in Spanish by Gabriel García Márquez.[2] This is not merely because I do not read Spanish, but also because this text exists as an object in itself that has been received as a novel in English by numerous ordinary readers, critics, and even scholars. It has been successful as a novel in English, and I think part of its success depends on a felicitous interrelationship between form and content.

Read as a novel in English by readers who do not even know for sure where the action takes place—perhaps somewhere in Latin

---

1. Gregory Rabassa, *One Hundred Years of Solitude* (New York: Avon, 1971). Subsequent quotations are from this edition.

2. Gabriel García Márquez, *Cien Años de Soledad* (Buenos Aires: Editorial Sudamericana, 1967).

America, or is there a part of coastal Spain that is like that?—
it is clear that the basic content of the novel is that life and death
are the same thing. One is born to die, and all of life is a movement
toward that goal. The biggest problem is to while away your time
while getting from birth to death. In doing this, you get carried
away with all sorts of diversions that seem important to you at
the time, but that in retrospect are ridiculous. Fortunately, we
are sexual beings, so a considerable amount of our time and energy
can be expended in adolescent yearning for erotic excitement,
mature abandon in sexual excess, and senile wonderment as to
what the hell it was all about. There is also entrepreneurship,
leadership, exploration, the founding of communities and societies,
the search for knowledge and entertainment, magic and science,
and war. In the end you discover that one endeavor is like any
other. You succeed, you fail, and then you succeed and fail again,
in the same thing, in something else, it really does not matter.
Life goes on and death is inevitable.

And because life and death are the same, neither does it matter
much whether you are dead or alive. Even if you are dead you
can hang around a long time and have an influence on the living.
The other side of that is that you need not give someone up just
because that person is dead; you can have commerce and
conversations with the dead just as much as with the living.

Part of this is because each of us incorporates our ancestors.
It is not just that all activities are intrinsically the same and one
as trivial as another. During the one hundred chronicled years
of the Buendia family, the same people keep getting born over
and over again, to repeat lives over and over again. You learn
that everything is repeated, over and over again, the people, the
places, the events.

And none of it means a goddamned thing. It is not just that
all human endeavors are absurd because they have no meaning
beyond themselves. It just does not matter what anyone does.
Even the attempt to keep body and soul together, as I remark

above, is not really necessary. Even the demand to get what one wants is never very urgent, because one sees soon enough that today's uncompromisable desire will be tomorrow's curiosity, yesterday's madness incomprehensible today. It is good to succeed, but failure has its compensations, and in the long run does not look much different from success. One way or another, life goes on and death is inevitable.

What holds everything together in *One Hundred Years of Solitude* is the personality of Ursula, who is blind through half the novel. Nobody notices, and it does not hinder her ability to follow what is going on, because nothing changes. When she dies, the twisted tale ends.

It is a pig's tail. I do not know if the same ambiguity hangs on a Spanish pig's behind, and I am not going to look it up. I hope you can go from tail to tale in Spanish, because if you cannot, then the English novel is that much better than the Spanish.

The narrative is a tale with a tail on both ends. It begins with incestuous love resulting in the birth of a son with a pig's tail, and ends with incestuous love resulting in the birth of a son with a pig's tail. This rounds out the tale, which begins where it ends, and ends where it begins. The basic form of the novel, then, is a circle.

The novel also contains many epicycles. Repetition of people is most obvious. Aurelianos are withdrawn, but upright and reliable when duty calls. José Arcadios are outgoing and wild, but not as reliable as you might suspect. Like Plato's globular urhuman, the Buendia male is split in half. Twins get mixed up. They may not go through life even with their right names, and they get buried in each other's graves. All opposites are the same. Aureliano is José Arcadio. Life is death.

In the heart of the novel are the epicyclic little golden fishes. It is not just that they get made and then melted down over and over (content), but that the story of their getting made and melted down, and of other things getting built and torn down and built up again, keeps getting repeated over and over again (form). Little golden fishes, Aurelianos, José Arcadios, funeral wreaths, shrouds, and little pig tails.

José Arcadio Buendia's dream of going from one identical room to another is an infinity of epicycles:

> He liked to go from room to room. As in a gallery of parallel mirrors, until Prudencio Aguilar would touch him on the shoulder. Then he would go back from room to room, walking in reverse, going back over his trail, and he would find Prudencio Aguilar in the room of reality. But one night, two weeks after they took him to his bed, Prudencio Aguilar touched his shoulder in an intermediate room and he stayed there forever, thinking it was the real room. (p. 137)

Of course it *was* the real room because they are all the same and it doesn't make any difference. This provides structural support in the text for the sameness of life and death in the novel. Going from the same room to the same room *ad infinitum* is the same as going in a circle, or nowhere. Everyone always goes in a circle. And stays there.

Here is a final epicycle. Colonel Aureliano dies standing under the chestnut tree with his head propped against the trunk. If his father's body is not buried under that tree, at least his ghost is still rotting there, so the circle goes from the ghost of Colonel Aureliano's father through the ground, into the tree, from the tree trunk into Colonel Aureliano's forehead down through his body to his feet to the ground again. What is more, the critical tool that opens and closes the story is hanging out, for Colonel Aureliano dies in the business of pissing on his father's ghost, which he has been doing over and over again for a very long time. There's a pig's tale for you.

The central circular image of the novel is presented at the

death of Ursula's son José Arcadio. The umbilical cord of blood extends from José Arcadio to his mother, as once the umbilical cord extended from her to him. Here are birth and death the same, connected in a circle.

> As soon as José Arcadio closed the bedroom door the sound of a pistol shot echoed through the house. A trickle of blood came out under the door, crossed the living room, went out into the street, continued on a straight line across the uneven terraces, went down steps and climbed over curbs, passed along the Street of the Turks, turned a corner to the right and another to the left, made a right angle at the Buendia house, went in under the closed door, crossed through the parlor, hugging the walls so as not to stain the rugs, went on to the other living room, made a wide curve to avoid the dining room table, went along the porch with the begonias, and passed without being seen under Amaranta's chair as she gave an arithmetic lesson to Aureliano José, and went through the pantry and came out in the kitchen, where Ursula was getting ready to crack thirty-six eggs to make bread.
> "Holy Mother of God!" Ursula shouted. (pp. 129–30)

The great textual deliberateness of this death passage and of the passage describing Colonel Aureliano's death (pp. 246–250) creates form that carries content.

When José Arcadio Segunda says to Ursula, "What did you expect? . . . Time passes," she replies, "That's how it goes . . . but not so much." And, "When she said it she realized that she was giving the same reply that Colonel Aureliano Buendia had given in his death cell, and once again she shuddered with the evidence that time was not passing, as she had just admitted, but that it was turning in a circle" (p. 310).

The circles are drawn by repetition of "not so much" on pp.

123 and 310. Descriptions of incidents are repeated with near identical phraseology, as in the first sentence of the novel, "Many years later, as he faced the firing squad, Colonel Aureliano Buendia was to remember . . ." (p. 11), in the first sentence of the middle section of the novel, "Years later on his deathbed Aureliano Segunda would remember . . ." (p. 174), and near the end, "A few months later, at the hour of his death, Aureliano Segunda would remember . . ." (p. 315).

Form carries content in *One Hundred Years of Solitude*. At its end, the text is brought around to its beginning again. The tale's tail is thrust into its mouth, and the circle of eternal sameness of life and death is closed.